EVERYDAY
INSPIRATION
from
God's Word

Daily Encouragement
for Women

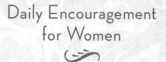

EVERYDAY
INSPIRATION
from
God's Word

BARBOUR BOOKS
An Imprint of Barbour Publishing, Inc.

© 2018 by Barbour Publishing, Inc.

Print ISBN 978-1-68322-578-2

eBook Editions:
Adobe Digital Edition (.epub) 978-1-68322-807-3
Kindle and MobiPocket Edition (.prc) 978-1-68322-808-0

Text originally appeared in the Today God Wants You to Know series: *You Are Blessed, You Are Loved, You Have a Purpose,* and *You Are Beautiful.* All published by Barbour Publishing.

Published by Barbour Books, an imprint of Barbour Publishing, Inc., 1810 Barbour Drive, Uhrichsville, Ohio 44683, www.barbourbooks.com

Our mission is to inspire the world with the life-changing message of the Bible.

Member of the
Evangelical Christian
Publishers Association

Printed in the United States of America.

INTRODUCTION

Your word is a lamp for my feet,
a light on my path.
PSALM 119:105 NIV

Where do you turn for inspiration? When you need a reminder of your worth, your purpose, your joy? The world tells us that we can find affirmation in our job, in our family, in a new item of clothing, or even in the number of likes we get on social media. But all of these things (even the good ones), are off the mark.

True encouragement, food for the heart and soul, comes from our Father God, in His Word. In this daily devotional you'll find bite-sized reminders of your worth, your purpose, your blessed life, and your beauty. . . . You are celebrated by the Creator of the universe who calls you by name.

Day 1
GOD'S ABUNDANCE

God is able to bless you abundantly.
2 CORINTHIANS 9:8 NIV

The literal meaning of these Greek words adds still another layer to our understanding of God's blessings. When Paul wrote this sentence to the Corinthians, he was talking about God's power—something that is over and above anything else we've ever encountered—to give grace and kindness to us that are also over and above anything we can even imagine. God's blessings are as abundant as His power to shower them upon us. None of our fears and doubts can ever limit either one!

Day 2
YOU ARE GOD'S FRIEND

---

*"I'm no longer calling you servants because
servants don't understand what their master
is thinking and planning. No, I've named
you friends because I've let you in on
everything I've heard from the Father."*

JOHN 15:15 MSG

❧

My best friend and I have known each other for
over two decades. We know each other's strengths,
faults, and weaknesses—and we still love to spend
time together.

God considers you His friend. He knows
everything about you, including your flaws, yet
He still loves you deeply. He wants to spend time
with you!

Day 3
FEARFULLY AND WONDERFULLY MADE

I will praise thee; for I am fearfully and
wonderfully made: marvellous are thy works.

PSALM 139:14 KJV

From time to time, most of us complain about
our bodies. Maybe our nose is too long, our eyes
too round, and our mouth too wide. We forget
that God's master plan specifically included our
features. When the psalmist suggests that we were
"fearfully made," he is telling us to consider our
bodies with a kind of reverence. We are looking at
God's handiwork. And He made no mistakes,
so maybe we should complain less and
praise more.

Day 4
FAVES AND RAVES

I delight to do Your will, O my God.
PSALM 40:8 NKJV

∼

Every one of us has a few favorite things, to quote the inimitable Julie Andrews. Rather than bright copper kettles, yours might be centered around coffee flavors, shoes, and lotions. We have favorite restaurants and events and holidays.

The psalmist said that his delight was an action. Put in a modern context, his delight was not just an Instagram photo of someone else's action; he delighted in *doing* God's will. Today, take a fresh look at God's law and then act on it. Let it become your new fave.

Day 5
THRIVING

I am like an olive tree, thriving in the house of God. I will always trust in God's unfailing love.

PSALM 52:8 NLT

❧

Children need love to thrive. So do all of us older folks. Without love, our hearts would be sad and lonely. Our lives would be narrow and unfulfilling. In fact, love is the most important of all the many spiritual blessings we've received. All God's blessings, both spiritual and physical, are wrapped up in His love. Because He loves us, He will never stop blessing us. His love never fails.

Day 6
YOU ARE CHOSEN

But you are a chosen race, a royal priesthood, a holy nation, a people for his own possession, that you may proclaim the excellencies of him who called you out of darkness into his marvelous light.

1 PETER 2:9 ESV

My mom and I used to hunt for Nancy Drew books at antiques stores. When I found a book I was hunting for, it was a thrill. I knew that chosen piece was special to me and unlike the rest.

In the same way, you've been handpicked for God's family. You are special to Him!

Day 7
WORKED IN SOMETHING GOOD

That's why we can be so sure that
every detail in our lives of love for God
is worked into something good.
ROMANS 8:28 MSG

Paul chose a very specific Greek word to convey the idea that the details of our lives (the good, the bad, and the ugly) all "work together" for our benefit. We get the English word *synergism* from this term. It means that all those details or circumstances cooperate or contribute toward God's stated goal. We certainly do not always understand what is being accomplished. But we can have confidence that it is being worked into something good.

Day 8
LOVE FOR BEAUTY

She makes tapestry for herself;
her clothing is fine linen and purple.
PROVERBS 31:22 NKJV

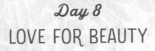

We don't know for sure just when women started caring about clothes. But a yearning for pretty clothing seems to be written on the very DNA of women.

The woman commended by God in Proverbs 31 wore fine clothing, made well and of the best color (purple was a luxury in that time).

God wants you to be beautiful by caring for yourself in the best manner you can. Honor His gift of femininity.

Day 9
BEAUTIFULLY OUTFITTED

Strength and honor are her clothing;
she shall rejoice in time to come.
PROVERBS 31:25 NKJV

Speaking of clothing. . .the beautiful woman of God has two items in her closet. Strength and honor. They are her basic wardrobe pieces, her essentials. She may accessorize with other things, but she is never without these.

They originate with God. He is the source of strength and the way to honor. Putting Him in first place ensures that these pieces of clothing are just your size.

And you will rejoice in the future because you wear them.

Day 10
SECURE

Such love has no fear, because perfect love expels all fear. If we are afraid, it is for fear of punishment.

1 JOHN 4:18 NLT

Sometimes love hurts. Even the people who love us most let us down—and we let them down. When we say or do the wrong thing, they may pull back from us. We fear we might lose their love. We worry they'll leave us, even if it's only through death. But God's love is perfect. It will never let us down. He never pulls away from us, no matter what we do. We are totally secure.

Day 11
YOU ARE NOT ALONE

For God has said, "I will never fail you. I will never abandon you."

HEBREWS 13:5 NLT

~

The older I get, the more I come across situations I have no idea how to handle. I think, *I just want someone to tell me what to do!*

One day, the Lord brought me to Hebrews 13:5, and I was reminded that God is with us through every situation we face. If we need help or direction, we can trust that voice on the inside to provide us with the right way to go.

Day 12
STRENGTHEN THE HAND OF A FRIEND

And Jonathan Saul's son arose, and went to David into the wood, and strengthened his hand in God.

1 SAMUEL 23:16 KJV

When you "strengthen someone's hand," you encourage them. You speak words of affirmation; you remind them of God's faithfulness and you urge them to immerse themselves in His grace. This Hebrew phrase carries the idea of directing someone to be courageous in spite of their circumstances. Like Jonathan, we all have friends who need to be encouraged. Look around. Whose hand can you strengthen today?

Day 13
WE ARE GOD'S KIDS

We are His people and the sheep of His pasture.
PSALM 100:3 NASB

～

The Beatles struck a chord when they sang, "All the lonely people, where do they all come from? All the lonely people, where do they all belong?" A sense of belonging is absolutely crucial to everyone's health and well-being. We need to have an emotional "home." The psalmist addresses that basic need and assures us that indeed we are God's. We belong to Him and "live and move and have our being" (Acts 17:28 NIV) in His pasture. Such comfort!

Day 14
QUIETED, BEAUTIFUL YOU

I sought the LORD, and He heard me,
and delivered me from all my fears.

PSALM 34:4 NKJV

Your fears make you uniquely you. They reveal what frightens you and show the shape of your personality. In your anxieties, the way your mind works is clearly seen.

Your fears do not put off the Master. He can handle them. He can soothe and calm your spirit. He sees the beauty within and wants to bring it out.

Give your fears to Him. You can be delivered.

Day 15
SIMPLY LOVE

God is love, and all who live in love live in God, and God lives in them.

1 JOHN 4:16 NLT

We often make our spiritual lives so complicated. We focus on theology. We believe our church has got it right, and we worry about those folks in the church down the road who have got it all wrong. But the Bible says it's really quite simple: when we live in love, we are living in God. God is living in us. His blessing flows through us and out into the world.

Day 16
YOU CAN BE PATIENT

---

*Instead, you will follow the example of those
who are going to inherit God's promises
because of their faith and endurance.*

HEBREWS 6:12 NLT

Because God loves you, you don't have to be
concerned about when you will see your prayers
answered. All you have to do is trust that they will
be answered.

In many situations we bring to the Lord, multiple
unknowns are in play—including the feelings and
prayers of other people. God is the only one who
sees everything and orchestrates life in a way that
only He can. Trust Him to do so.

Day 17
SPIRITUAL FOOTPRINTS

The things which you have heard from me. . .
entrust these to faithful men who will
be able to teach others also.

2 TIMOTHY 2:2 NASB

Recording a mother's spiritual journey is a powerful way to influence generations to come. Children can likely reiterate the tenets of our personal faith, but how can we influence grandchildren? How can we leave spiritual footprints? One way is to write in our Bibles and keep them for our families. Journaling will leave a trail of faith, and so will marking up a favorite hymnbook. Let's start thinking of ways to make the spiritual footprints obvious.

Day 18
PAST AND PRESENT BEAUTY

But Mary quietly treasured these things in
her heart and often thought about them.
LUKE 2:19 TLB

Every memory you have is colored by your
perception, your emotion, your vantage point. Your
memories, to a large degree, are you. We women
treasure memories of special days, events, and
emotions.

Today, God wants you to know that you are as
beautiful to Him as on that long-ago day when your
hair was coiffed and your dress was princess-like.
You wish for past beauty, but the reality is that to
Him, you are always lovely.

Day 19
STRONG HEARTS

---

*"Don't be dejected and sad, for the joy
of the LORD is your strength!"*

NEHEMIAH 8:10 NLT

The Hebrew word used in this verse is *chedvah*,
meaning "rejoicing, gladness." Depression weakens
our hearts and separates us from others. But we
have a relationship with the Creator of the universe,
and He shares His eternal gladness with us. His joy
makes us strong, able to face the challenges of life,
able to reach out to others. Just as God shares His
gladness with us, we are meant to share our
joy with everyone we meet.

Day 20
YOU CAN GIVE GOD TIME

Then he added, "Pay close attention to what you hear. The closer you listen, the more understanding you will be given—and you will receive even more."

MARK 4:24 NLT

❦

Have you ever started a conversation with someone who walked away halfway through your first sentence? It's as though they didn't hear you talk. Maybe they started the conversation but left before listening? Do you think God feels like that sometimes?

Do more than just quickly read the Bible or blurt out your prayer requests. Spend time with God. He wants to talk to you!

Day 21
A GOOD FIGHT

---

*"Put your minds on the Master,
great and awesome, and then fight for your
brothers, your sons, your daughters,
your wives, and your homes."*

NEHEMIAH 4:14 MSG

In context, this passage has to do with a physical fight regarding the wall in Jerusalem. But there are many other situations that need our diligent response. As wives and mothers, we are the keepers of our homes, and our children deserve our persistent protection. In this electronic age, it takes effort. Moms need to fight for the purity of their children. Turn off devices. Monitor things. Say no. Fight for the hearts of those you love. It matters.

Day 22
LEARNING FOR A LIFETIME

"Take My yoke upon you and learn from Me."
MATTHEW 11:29 NKJV

Tiled halls. Metal lockers. Loud bells. One-armed desks.

Remember your school days? What did you learn?

Hopefully, you are still benefiting from the days you spent in a classroom. Every one of them is a stroke on the canvas of your life, a contribution to the heart of your being. You're now in God's school of grace. He invites you to get in sync with Him and learn how to do things His way.

It's the way to beautiful living.

Day 23
LIFT UP YOUR VOICE!

They shall lift up their voice, they shall sing for
the majesty of the LORD, they shall cry aloud.
ISAIAH 24:14 KJV

❦

There's a lot of singing going on in the Old Testament! Here the Hebrew word *ranan* means a happiness that's expressed vocally, with shouts of joy, with loud singing. Unfortunately, we haven't all been blessed with beautiful singing voices—but we have all been blessed by God in ways that make us sing! Even if we can't carry a tune, He's glad to hear our voices lifted up in praise.

Day 24
YOU CAN MOVE MOUNTAINS

Elijah was as human as we are, and yet when
he prayed earnestly that no rain would fall,
none fell for three and a half years! Then,
when he prayed again, the sky sent down rain
and the earth began to yield its crops.

JAMES 5:17–18 NLT

～

Our prayers are backed up by the power of this
world's Creator. When we pray in faith, anything
can happen. Elijah had direction from God to pray
for rain; we have the Word of God. Pray the Word,
and watch it come to life!

Day 25
SIGNING OUR WORK

*Slack habits and sloppy work
are as bad as vandalism.*
PROVERBS 18:9 MSG

The story goes that the night before his sculpture the *Pietà* was to be unveiled, Michelangelo overheard some critics questioning whether it was really his work. So he went back into the studio and chiseled his entire name along the fold of Mary's garment. (You can see it when you visit Rome.) It is important to take pride in our work whether it is in a kitchen or a boardroom. Let's make sure and sign our names to everything we do. No slack habits!

Day 26
CRAZY INFATUATIONS

---

*"How beautiful you are,
my love, how beautiful!"*
SONG OF SOLOMON 4:1 TLB

~

"I've got a crush on you!"

Not many of us sang those words to the guy we daydreamed about, but there is hardly one of us who hasn't experienced the wild adrenaline rush, flushed cheeks, and erratic heartbeat that accompany an infatuation. Those feelings, in a small way, mirror the heart of a woman, our longings for a great romance.

Today, God wants you to know that He is the longing behind every crush you ever had, and that makes you beautiful to Him.

Day 27
INEXPRESSIBLE

You love him even though you have never seen him. . . . You trust him; and you rejoice with a glorious, inexpressible joy.

1 PETER 1:8 NLT

From the world's perspective, it might seem as though Jesus is our imaginary friend. After all, we can't see Him, can't hear Him. But we know His presence is real because He has blessed us with a joy that lies beyond words. *Aneklálētos* is the word Peter uses here, a joy that's impossible to convey with words. It can't be grasped with language, can't be pinned down with any of our human concepts. But it's real!

Day 28
YOU CAN PRAY FOR YOUR FAMILY

*That he would grant you, according to the riches
of his glory, to be strengthened with might
by his Spirit in the inner man.*

EPHESIANS 3:16 KJV

❧

The routine of living with someone can unintentionally cause us to forget that our family needs prayer too. In particular, we should provide the strongest prayer support for our husbands. Even if you're not yet married, start praying for him!

If you don't know what to pray, go to the Bible. There you'll find prayers to say for family that will encourage you in the process.

Day 29
AFFIRMING OUR WORK

And let the loveliness of our Lord, our God,
rest on us, confirming the work that we do.
Oh, yes. Affirm the work that we do!
PSALM 90:17 MSG

When we ask God to affirm our work, we are literally asking Him to let it stand in an upright position or be noted as steadfast. It is set in place and by extension has value and worth. It's not just something we do to pay the rent. With God's stamp of approval, our work is important and established as a meaningful pursuit.

Day 30
TRAVELS

He shall have dominion also from sea to sea,
and from the River to the ends of the earth.
PSALM 72:8 NKJV

❧

Pack your bag and go!

There is exhilaration in seeing new places, eating different foods, and walking unknown paths. Those of us who like to wander a bit may be assured that the magnificence of every exotic place on earth is only a shadow compared to the beauty our God built in the very essence of who we are.

Whether you're sitting on a plane or by your own fireplace, think about that right now.

Day 31
FORGET FEAR

"*Go in peace. Your journey has
the Lord's approval.*"

JUDGES 18:6 NIV

In this verse, *shalom* means freedom from fear. We may not fear for our physical safety, but we often live with a constant, nagging anxiety, a sense that doom and gloom is hanging over us and the people we love. God wants to take that anxiety away from us. The word translated here as "approval" means literally "to go in front of." Knowing God precedes us into the future, we can let go of all our worries. We can go in peace.

Day 32
WHOLE

And He said to her, "Daughter, your faith has made you well; go in peace and be healed."

MARK 5:34 NASB

In the New Testament, instead of the Hebrew word *shalom*, we have the Greek word *eiréné*. Much like *shalom*, its meaning is far deeper than simply freedom from conflict. This peace means that all the essential parts of our lives are joined together. It means that we have been healed, body and soul. All the broken pieces of our hearts have been put back together. In Christ, we have been made whole.

Day 33
YOU DON'T HAVE TO KNOW WHY

Trust God from the bottom of your heart;
don't try to figure out everything on your own.
PROVERBS 3:5 MSG

Recently, I saw a blackout curtain on sale while shopping. *Buy it.* This distinct thought felt God-given, but because I didn't understand why I needed the curtain, I didn't buy it.

Within a day, I realized my kids were waking up early because the sun was too bright in their room. Back to the store I went, remembering again that I don't have to understand what the Holy Spirit tells me. All I have to do is obey.

Day 34
RESULTS

Throw yourselves into the work of the Master,
confident that nothing you do for him
is a waste of time or effort.
1 CORINTHIANS 15:58 MSG

Regardless of the kind of career we have (in the living room or a boardroom), we pray that it matters and that our effort counts for something. That's why Paul assured the Corinthians that their work was not a waste of time. The Greek term means "to be full." When our work is done for God, it's full of meaning; it is fruitful. So let's throw ourselves into our jobs this week and watch Him bless them.

Day 35
AGE DOESN'T MATTER

Charm and grace are deceptive, and beauty is
vain [because it is not lasting], but a woman
who reverently and worshipfully fears
the Lord, she shall be praised!

PROVERBS 31:30 AMPC

❧

Aging is not supposed to be beautiful. It is, after all, a fading of our vibrancy and tautness, a decline into less color and more sags. No woman longs for that.

God's Word tells us that earthly physical beauty isn't lasting. We must cement our identity not in how we look but in who He is in us.

And His eyes see your essence anyway, regardless of the skin.

Day 36
BLESSED BY GOD

And God blessed them.
GENESIS 1:22 KJV

ک

In the very first chapter of the first book of the
Bible, we read that God was already in the business
of blessing. He created the world—and then He
blessed it. But what are we talking about when we
use that familiar word, _blessing_? Did you ever stop
to think what it means to be blessed?

Day 37
YOU ARE UNIQUE

"Before I formed you in the womb I knew you,
and before you were born I consecrated you;
I appointed you a prophet to the nations."
JEREMIAH 1:5 ESV

No one else in the world is just like you. Your hair, your eyes, your looks. Your personality, your smile, your charm. Absolutely everything about you is special. God created you to be exactly who you are.

When self-doubt surfaces, think about what makes you special. Know that God has made you as He did for a reason. You can embrace your beauty.

Day 38
IT HAS ALREADY BEEN GIVEN TO US

*Everything that goes into a life of pleasing God
has been miraculously given to us by getting
to know, personally and intimately,
the One who invited us to God.*

2 PETER 1:3 MSG

Stop the struggle. We have already been given all that we need for this life and the one to come. Christ has arranged for it all. Our job is just to stay connected to Him. We connect through prayer, meditation, and Bible reading. We see His face as we serve. We already have all the tools necessary to accomplish His will in our lives. We just need to use them.

Day 39
EBB AND FLOW

You chart the path ahead of me and tell me where to stop and rest. Every moment you know where I am. You know what I am going to say before I even say it.

PSALM 139:3–4 TLB

❧

God understands you. Your thoughts. Your emotions. Your longings. What prompts them. He is intimately acquainted with all your ways. He knows how you ride the wave of feeling and that sometimes you sense you're going under the crest instead of over. But He wants you to believe that He sees beauty in the depths of you and that no tide of emotion can drown it.

Day 40
SIXFOLD BLESSINGS

"I will be with you and bless you."
GENESIS 26:3 NLT

Merriam-Webster's Dictionary gives six definitions for *bless*:

1. to hallow or consecrate
2. to invoke divine care for
3. to praise or glorify
4. to give happiness and prosperity
5. to protect and preserve
6. to endow with a gift

God blesses you in all these ways. You are set aside to be God's dwelling place—and that makes you sacred. Through Christ, you have the right to ask God for help and care. He speaks to you; He gives you happiness and health; He protects you; and He gives you countless gifts!

Day 41
BOTH FAR AND NEAR

"Am I a God who is only close at hand?" says the
LORD. "No, I am far away at the same time. . . .
Am I not everywhere in all the heavens and earth?"

JEREMIAH 23:23–24 NLT

❧

Some people say God is too holy to be present
in the ordinary world, while others insist He is
in nature, in human faces, in our own minds and
bodies. In this verse, God says, "You're both right!
I'm right here with you—*and* I'm far too great to be
contained by your small world. But it doesn't
matter. Far or near, I am everywhere!"

Day 42
FRUITFUL BLESSINGS

"I will bless him, and will make him fruitful."

GENESIS 17:20 NASB

∽

In this verse, the Hebrew word that we've translated *bless* has to do with making something bear fruit. God blesses us by making our lives productive; we create homes and gardens, we raise children and help others; we write stories, paint pictures, and make music. That's one kind of fruitfulness He gives us. He also, however, makes our spirits bear a different kind of fruit—joy, humility, peace, understanding, and most of all, love.

Day 43
YOU CAN BRING HEAVEN TO EARTH

*"May your Kingdom come soon. May your will
be done on earth, as it is in heaven."*

MATTHEW 6:10 NLT

God wants you to be a part of His work on earth. He longs for you to exercise your faith in His will. This is because God has included us in His plans through our prayers. Our prayers enable us to access God in heaven. What a privilege!

If you want something from heaven to come to earth, pray. Entreat God to make it happen.

Day 44
SET APART

"Before I formed you in the womb I knew you,
before you were born I set you apart."
JEREMIAH 1:5 NIV

·~·

"To be set apart" carries the idea of being "ordained." The Hebrew word is used about 2,000 times in the Old Testament and means to be "literally placed." In the same way, God set the stars in the sky (Genesis 1:17) and a rainbow in the clouds (Genesis 9:13); He has literally placed us on a course before we were even born. Being set aside for a very specific purpose is a goal worth pursuing.

Day 45
BIRTHDAY SUITED

But God gives to it the body that He plans and sees fit, and to each kind of seed a body of its own.
1 CORINTHIANS 15:38 AMPC

⤳

Apple or pear? Top-heavy, bottom-heavy, or stick-figured?

Oh, we women labor under these vivid illustrations of our bodies! And we feel shamed for our DNA-imprinted shape, which we didn't choose.

Girlfriend, you aren't responsible for the bones. Only the meat on them. The basic structure was chosen by God, and the seed that is the real you is most important anyway.

Love it and go with it! Beautify your world!

Day 46
ALREADY BLESSED

God. . .has blessed us in the heavenly realms
with every spiritual blessing in Christ.
EPHESIANS 1:3 NIV

⸎

That's pretty amazing. Right now, in the world of eternity—the spiritual world—you and I already possess all that God has to give to us. We don't have to wait for these blessings. We don't have to wait until we die and go to heaven. We don't have to earn them first, and we don't have to work hard to become "more spiritual." They're already ours, right now.

Day 47
YOU CAN ENJOY GOD'S WORD

All Scripture is inspired by God and is useful to teach us what is true and to make us realize what is wrong in our lives. It corrects us when we are wrong and teaches us to do what is right.

2 TIMOTHY 3:16 NLT

❧

Reading the Bible can be intimidating, but only when you don't understand its purpose. The Bible has the power to do amazing things in us. If you have trouble reading the Word, ask the Holy Spirit to help. He'll make the Bible come alive for you!

Day 48
GOD HAS A DETAILED PROGRAM

---

*I will exalt You, I will give thanks to Your name;
for You have worked wonders, plans formed
long ago, with perfect faithfulness.*
ISAIAH 25:1 NASB

Hannibal Smith (from the TV series *The A-Team*)
often said that he loved it when a plan came together.
So do we. We want to know that all the circumstances
of life have meaning, that they are part of a grand
scheme. Isaiah affirms God's plans and remarks that
they were formed long ago. There is amazing comfort
in knowing God considered our lives a very long
time ago. Clearly, He is in control.

Day 49
THE LOST ART

A gracious woman retains honor.
PROVERBS 11:16 NKJV

❧

The art of graciousness is somewhat lost today. We know how to be cool (what used to be called "hip"), and some even yearn for the unbecoming, seductive title of "hot." But being gracious doesn't seem very popular among today's women. It might be appropriate for the queen of England but definitely not for a young woman who wants to have beauty. Right?

Actually, no. It is a description for any woman, every woman; it is the essence of refined femininity and decorum. We need to return to it.

Day 50
FOR AS LONG AS IT TAKES!

---

*Love is patient, love is kind. . .bears all things,
believes all things, hopes all things,
endures all things.*

1 CORINTHIANS 13:4, 7 NASB

~

We usually think of these verses as a description
of how we should love others (which, of course,
they are). But these familiar words also describe
how God loves us. He is patient with us, no matter
how many times we fall on our faces, no matter how
long we take to learn something. He never stops
believing in us. He's willing to put up with us for
as long as it takes!

Day 51
YOU DON'T HAVE TO SOLVE EVERYONE'S PROBLEMS

And let us consider how we may spur one another on toward love and good deeds.

HEBREWS 10:24 NIV

∽

I often think my way is the best and everyone should follow it. When a problem arises, if everyone listened to me, they'd be fine.

That's a rather lofty position to take. Solving everyone's problems isn't my job, particularly because I know only one side of the story. I cannot force anyone to choose God, but I can encourage people to move toward Him.

Day 52
WORK, AND WE GET TO EAT

He who tills his land will have plenty of bread,
but he who pursues worthless things lacks sense.
PROVERBS 12:11 NASB

In Hebrew, a worthless thing is empty. It is hollow and without meaning. Too often, we avoid hard work and get distracted by all manner of silliness. This wise proverb is making a clear statement regarding employment: if you work, you get to eat. No work, no food. It's a basic but powerful motivator. Since we all like to eat, it's a good time to pause and thank the Lord for our work.

Day 53
BEAUTIFUL BUILDERS

The wise woman builds her house,
but the foolish pulls it down with her hands.

PROVERBS 14:1 NKJV

Many of us know the parable Jesus told about the wise man and the foolish man. We sang the Sunday school song about building on the rock or on the sand. But did you know that there are wise and foolish women too?

These women either build up or tear down their homes with their own hands. Through attitude, words, choices, and priorities a woman can demonstrate whether she is a builder or a demolitionist.

Which are you?

Day 54
OVERFLOWING JOY

I am exceeding joyful in all our tribulation.
2 CORINTHIANS 7:4 KJV

Paul confirms what Jesus already told His followers: in the midst of trouble, when no one understands us, when problems are everywhere we turn, we are blessed with joy! This joy isn't something small and weak, and it isn't merely a stiff-upper-lip endurance. Instead, the Greek word *chara* means joy that's abundant, overflowing—joy so great it can't even be measured. God's blessings are never limited by human problems—and He does nothing by half-measures!

Day 55
YOU DON'T HAVE TO WEAR SOMEONE ELSE'S ARMOR

---

*Then Saul gave David his own armor. . . .
"I can't go in these," [David] protested
to Saul. "I'm not used to them."
So David took them off again.*

1 SAMUEL 17:38–39 NLT

We can easily assume people need to live and pray as we do, just as King Saul assumed David must dress for battle as he did.

Trust God to show you the path He wants you to walk. It may look different from others, but as long as it is aligned with God's Word, follow your heart.

Day 56
I LOVE MY JOB

Whatever you do, do your work heartily,
as for the Lord rather than for men.
COLOSSIANS 3:23 NASB

Instead of taking careful notes, a court reporter sat for months typing "I hate my job" over and over again. Needless to say, once he was caught, it totally disrupted the flow of legal proceedings, and cases had to be retried. We might not be actually typing that sentiment, but women may be silently mouthing, "I hate my job" too. Paul wanted to encourage us all to see our work as a kind of worship unto the Lord. So try it. . . . "I love my job, I love my job."

EVERY SINGLE DAY

"As long as the earth remains, there will be
springtime and harvest, cold and heat,
winter and summer, day and night."
GENESIS 8:22 TLB

Do you have a favorite season?

Today, whatever season of the year it is outside, you are on God's mind. In the spring, He likes you in pastels. In the summer, He delights in your joy of going barefoot. In the fall, He looks at you with love in your sweater and scarf. And in the winter, He smiles at the snowflakes in your hair.

Every single day of the year you are His beloved.

Day 58
TAUGHT BY GOD

---

*I will instruct you and teach you in the way
which you should go; I will counsel
you with My eye upon you.*

PSALM 32:8 NASB

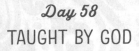

One spiritual blessing that we're promised is God's guidance. This seldom means that we hear His voice speaking clearly, directly. He doesn't write His directions in big letters across the sky. Instead, He teaches us—and teaching is a process that's often long and slow. We have so much to learn, but God sees our lives clearly, and He has promised to teach us everything we need to know.

Day 59
ABLE TO LAUGH

A merry heart doeth good like a medicine.
PROVERBS 17:22 KJV

My Aunt Missy shines with God's love, partially because she can always laugh at herself. A favorite story was when she was driving a convertible around a cul-de-sac and recognized her friend's parents walking nearby. She couldn't remember their names, so she waved and yelled what she did remember. . .her own name. They looked at her oddly and smiled. Her embarrassment has become a story she loves to tell.

Go ahead and laugh at yourself; it's one way you can be a bright light for Jesus.

Day 60
LOVE ONE ANOTHER

*"A new command I give you:
Love one another."*

JOHN 13:34 NIV

C. S. Lewis once remarked, "Affection is responsible for nine tenths of whatever solid and durable happiness there is in our lives." And he is so right. Jesus commanded us to love one another. And every mother knows it takes affection to express our love. It takes a touch, a word, a kindness, a gift of any size, a tone of voice, or a smile. If we want to be happy, really happy, we must begin today to love others.

Day 61
RAINY DAYS

*"He gives rain on the earth,
and sends waters on the fields."*

JOB 5:10 NKJV

Karen Carpenter crooned, "Rainy days and Mondays always get me down."

Maybe you feel like that. Perhaps the gray skies and sloshy puddles make you feel sad. Or maybe you relish a good rainy day now and then, enjoying a bowl of soup and a favorite book. God knows which is your tendency. And He wants to be part of every rainy day you have. Trust Him when the clouds start to roll in. He is still watching out for you.

Day 62
WORDLESS PRAISE

The beast of the field shall honour me. . .
because I give waters in the wilderness,
and rivers in the desert.

ISAIAH 43:20 KJV

Deer and woodchucks, chipmunks and rabbits, snakes and spiders, dragonflies and prairie dogs: each creature in its own way praises and honors God. Wordlessly, even without human intelligence and reasoning, they show us that God provides for His creation even in the most barren lands. His blessings reach into the wild, secret places. He forgets none of His creation and blesses it all.

Day 63
ABLE TO GO OUTSIDE
YOUR COMFORT ZONE

---

*"Go into all the world and preach
the Good News to everyone."*

MARK 16:15 NLT

My friend Colleen is quiet and reserved until she
shares Jesus with others. One time, she walked up
to a group of guys playing soccer. The ball came
toward her. She stepped on it, encouraged the
guys to come over, shared about Jesus, prayed with
them, then let them continue their game.

Just as Colleen did, you can rely on the
Holy Spirit to help you boldly share the
Gospel with others.

Day 64
TODAY'S SCHEDULE

Whatever you do, do it all for the glory of God.
1 CORINTHIANS 10:31 NIV

In *Alice in Wonderland*, Alice asks the Cheshire Cat for advice: "Which road should I take?" The Cat replies, "Where are you going?" Alice says she doesn't know, and the Cat replies, "If you don't know where you are going, any road will get you there." Any old road doesn't work for God's daughters. Let's look at our schedules for today and choose those things that lead to His glory.

Day 65
THROUGH AND THROUGH

*For the word of God is living and powerful,
and sharper than any two-edged sword,
piercing even to the division of soul and spirit,
and of joints and marrow, and is a discerner
of the thoughts and intents of the heart.*

HEBREWS 4:12 NKJV

Have you ever been around a woman who was beautiful to you until you saw her motives? Someone with gorgeous features can be driven by hideous, selfish, conniving desires.

God wants us to be lovely through and through. He has given us His Word to show us where we need His power to make us that way.

Day 66
WORSHIP

*"Worthy are You, our Lord and our God,
to receive glory and honor and power;
for You created all things, and because of
Your will they existed, and were created."*

REVELATION 4:11 NASB

❧

Enjoying the blessings of nature is also a form of worship. The awe and delight we feel when we see a towering mountain, a storm-tossed ocean, or a field of wildflowers can turn our hearts to God. When that happens, we're caught in another blessing circle: the more we worship God through nature's blessings, the more we are blessed!

Day 67
ABLE TO SEE THEIR NEED

For the LORD gives wisdom; from his mouth come knowledge and understanding.

PROVERBS 2:6 NIV

A mom makes sure her kids are fed and well rested so they don't get crabby. A friend brings a meal to a grieving wife or lends a listening ear. A cousin calls to check on her family member whose parents just got divorced. One way we reflect Jesus to the world is by looking for other people's needs and doing everything we can to meet them.

Ask God: Whose need can I meet today?

Day 68
PUT POCKETS

For unto whomsoever much is given,
of him shall be much required.

LUKE 12:48 KJV

೨

A while back, it seems that England was inundated with pickpockets. Some Londoners wanted to protect their international reputation as a friendly city, so they organized themselves and began putting money *into* visitors' pockets. *Time* magazine called these generous people "put pockets." It seems that these folks stumbled onto an important spiritual principle. It goes like this: If you have, then give. So, would you like to be a put pocket? Whom can you bless today?

Day 69
HE HOLDS THE MIRROR

And such were some of you. But you were washed,
but you were sanctified, but you were justified
in the name of the Lord Jesus and
by the Spirit of our God.

1 CORINTHIANS 6:11 NKJV

Those who belong to Christ have been changed.
Maybe in the past you have had unhealthy views
of your identity and your need to attract the eyes
and desires of men. But when Christ holds the
mirror for us, we can look in it and see the truth
that we are changed. His love and approval
are now the standard for our beauty.

Day 70
THE BLESSING OF FRIENDSHIP

A friend loves at all times,
and a brother is born for adversity.

PROVERBS 17:17 NASB

When things are going our way, we may be tempted to think we are so strong that we don't need anyone's help. We may consider ourselves so spiritually mature that we can go it alone, "just me and the Lord." But sooner or later, all of us face times when everything seems to fall apart. We can't cope with life, and even our faith falters. When a friend quietly offers us her hand, that's the moment when we truly understand the blessing of friendship!

Day 71
IMMERSE YOURSELF IN GRACE

*"Don't pick on people, jump on their failures,
criticize their faults—unless, of course,
you want the same treatment.
That critical spirit has a
way of boomeranging."*
MATTHEW 7:1–2 MSG

~

After hearing news that another celebrity marriage ended after only four years, I thought, *That's dumb.* Then I immediately heard inside me, *"That's difficult."*

God hasn't called me to judge other people's decisions. My job is to love them, recognize I don't understand their situation, and give them grace upon grace for what they are facing.

Day 72
WE HAVE EVERYTHING WE NEED

His divine power has given us
everything we need for a godly life.
2 PETER 1:3 NIV

Before we start a project, we need to make sure
we have all the materials at hand. There is nothing
worse than being halfway through a recipe and
realizing you don't have the correct spice. But in life,
God has made certain that we have everything we
need to serve others. Our personality, our spiritual
gift set, our life circumstances perfectly match the
work at hand. All excuses are gone. Whom do you
need to serve today?

Day 73
SET-APART BEAUTY

*Therefore if anyone cleanses himself from
the latter, he will be a vessel for honor,
sanctified and useful for the Master,
prepared for every good work.*

2 TIMOTHY 2:21 NKJV

To be sanctified is to be set apart, made ready for
a sacred purpose. God wants not only to justify us
(forgive our sins), but also to sanctify us, to make
us holy and ready for His use.

Much of the beauty in our world today is self-
absorbed and self-gratifying. We are to be different.

Today, surrender your beauty to Him
and discover the joy of being set apart,
sanctified.

Day 74
DON'T FORGET TO SAY THANK YOU

I always thank my God for you.
1 CORINTHIANS 1:4 NLT

When you thank God for the many blessings He has given you, don't forget the people He has put in your life. Thank Him for your friends and your family, your coworkers and your employers. Thank Him for the people you know casually and for each stranger you pass on the street. Thank Him even for the difficult people you encounter! Each and every one of them can be a vehicle for God's blessing to flow into your life.

ENCOURAGE ONE ANOTHER

---

*And then there will be one huge family reunion
with the Master. So reassure one
another with these words.*

1 THESSALONIANS 4:17–18 MSG

❦

The Chicago preacher D. L. Moody once encouraged his congregation by remarking, "Soon you will read in the newspaper that I am dead. Don't believe it for a moment. I will be more alive than ever before." That is what Paul is asserting in this verse. There is a great family reunion coming, and we ought to regularly remind one another of that fact. Go encourage a friend.

Day 76
NOT A FRAGILE SENTIMENT

"I am leaving you with a gift—peace of mind and heart! And the peace I give isn't fragile like the peace the world gives. So don't be troubled or afraid."

JOHN 14:27 TLB

Womanhood is an assignment.

You are called to live on this earth as a female bearer of God's image, to interact with others and glorify Him through that template. He has given you personal beauty and a womanly perspective as well as the wondrous treasure of His peace—not a fragile, wispy sentiment but a stable, supportive assurance that will go with you and keep you.

Day 77
SPEED-OF-LIGHT BLESSINGS

God is our refuge and strength,
an ever-present help in trouble.
PSALM 46:1 NIV

The Hebrew word that's been translated *ever-present* is an interesting one. It carries within it several meanings: something that's diligent and never gives up; something unbelievably fast; something that shouts louder than any other sound. That's the way God's blessings reach us when we're in trouble—unstoppable, breaking the sound barrier, faster than the speed of light. No matter how big the problem, His help will be there when we need it.

Day 78
HE IS FLEXIBLE

Wait on the LORD: be of good courage,
and he shall strengthen thine heart:
wait, I say, on the LORD.
PSALM 27:14 KJV

∽

Religion says we must have a quiet time of thirty minutes every morning to grow close to God, but God is flexible. If reading the Bible in the morning is intimidating, try reading in the afternoon or evening. Listen to the Bible while driving. Read this devotional while waiting for an oil change.

Whatever you do, keep your goal in mind: being continually aware of and strengthening your relationship with God.

Day 79
FRUIT OF THE SPIRIT

But what happens when we live God's way?
He brings gifts into our lives, much the same
way that fruit appears in an orchard—things like
affection for others, exuberance about life, serenity.
GALATIANS 5:22 MSG

The Lord orders the life of a believer. He has a plan for us. And when we live out that plan, He rewards us with a spiritual harvest. He calls that the "fruit of the Spirit." Personal peace is part of that fruit. But remember, that peace or serenity is hinged on obedience. We need to keep saying yes to the Lord every single day.

Day 80
CLEAR VISION; BEAUTIFUL REVELATIONS

For now we see through a glass, darkly; but then face to face: now I know in part; but then shall I know even as also I am known.

1 CORINTHIANS 13:12 KJV

The best we can do down here is a smudgy reflection of God's glory. Our best youthful beauty is like peering into the tarnished silver of an antique mirror. It's not very clear.

But one day we will see Him face-to-face, and our eyes will be fully opened to see the majesty of that glory revealed in us as we never saw it on earth.

Day 81
HEART'S DESIRE

Take delight in the LORD, and he will
give you the desires of your heart.

PSALM 37:4 NIV

Sometimes it feels as though we have an empty place inside us that can never be filled, no matter how many things we get. That empty place is real, but material possessions can never fill it up. The Bible says that God put eternity into our hearts. Deep inside our innermost beings we yearn for all that eternity holds, all its abundance and beauty. Only God can give us the deepest, real desires of our hearts.

Day 82
FIGHT DISTRACTION

*Their loyalty is divided between God and the world,
and they are unstable in everything they do.*

JAMES 1:8 NLT

From friends and family to media and social media,
a lot of voices in this world are clamoring for your
attention. If you listen to them, you will find your
life to be unstable. Aim to keep your ears tuned in
to the voice that matters most: our heavenly Father.
As you tune in to Him and tune out others, you'll
hear the Lord's voice more clearly.

Day 83
HIS PARTING GIFT

"That's my parting gift to you. Peace. I don't leave you the way you're used to being left—feeling abandoned, bereft. So don't be upset."

JOHN 14:27 MSG

༄

The most significant gift anyone could ever be given is the peace of God. The night before He died, Christ made sure His disciples understood that truth. He promised to never leave them alone. He promised to be with them in all circumstances. And He promised them a gift, a confident assurance that could structure and give meaning to their entire life. He promised them (and us) His peace. Are you leaning into it today?

Day 84
TEARS WIPED AWAY

And God shall wipe away all tears from their eyes;
and there shall be no more death, neither sorrow,
nor crying, neither shall there be any more pain:
for the former things are passed away.

REVELATION 21:4 KJV

The ability to cry is a human gift. The body is capable of expressing what is going on inside, proving the interconnectedness of the physical and emotional parts of us.

Some tears are ones of joy; but mostly, tears denote sorrow. And God is going to eliminate sorrow from our eternal existence. Won't that be beautiful?

Day 85
JOHN 3:16

For God so loved the world, that he gave his only begotten Son, that whosoever believeth in him should not perish, but have everlasting life.

JOHN 3:16 KJV

If you grew up going to Sunday school, you probably know this verse by heart. The words may have become *too* familiar, so take a moment to think about what this verse really means. It's the message of the Gospel all wrapped up in a nutshell: God loves you...God gives you His Son...through Jesus you have life...in Him you'll never die.

Day 86
FIGHT THE ENEMY

For we are not fighting against flesh-and-blood enemies, but against evil rulers and authorities of the unseen world, against mighty powers in this dark world, and against evil spirits in the heavenly places.

EPHESIANS 6:12 NLT

༄

We often focus our mental energies and frustrations on the people around us since we interact regularly with them—yet they are not our enemy. Our enemy is Satan and his cohorts. Whenever people frustrate us, step back. No person is our enemy. Instead, look to God, and He will give you wisdom for the situation you face.

Day 87
SUBMISSION

"Submit to God and be at peace with him."

JOB 22:21 NIV

❧

Other translations of this verse suggest that we should "yield" or "acquaint ourselves" with God, and then we can be at peace with Him. The idea is to be so familiar with Him and His ways that getting in step is easy. When we understand His directions and "go with the flow," our burdens are lifted and our attitudes are encouraged. Listen carefully—you can almost hear Him calling cadence as we march along. Let the peace settle in.

Day 88
HIS CREATIVITY IN YOU

When I consider Your heavens, the work of Your fingers, the moon and the stars, which You have ordained, what is man that You are mindful of him, and the son of man that You visit him?

PSALM 8:3–4 NKJV

Think how incredibly awesome it was of God to write the witness of His glory in things that are visible!

The vast heavens, the celestial bodies—they all blaze with the message of His creative presence.

You, with your God-given beauty and your grace-filled life, are a witness to it as well.

Today, you are the star; shine!

Day 89
CHANGED PRIORITIES

"Don't be so concerned about perishable things like food. Spend your energy seeking the eternal life that the Son of Man can give you."

JOHN 6:27 NLT

ও

If we could just remember that we live both inside and outside time, in the same eternal realm with Jesus, we'd stop worrying so much about whether we'll have enough in this world. Our perspective would shift; our priorities would change. We'd live in the stream of never-ending blessing that is God's life, our eyes fixed on Jesus.

FIGHT CLOSED EARS

My child, listen and be wise:
keep your heart on the right course.
PROVERBS 23:19 NLT

Recently, my husband wanted me to make cookies with him. Based on my lengthy to-do list, I said no. After two more attempts, he said, "I was trying to relive some of our memories baking together in the kitchen."

Being too busy with good things is an easy trap to fall into, so resolve to take time to listen to cues from your family and friends. If they need you, put them first.

Day 91
CHERISHING GOD'S WORD

Thy law is my delight.
PSALM 119:174 KJV

～

One of the artifacts recovered from Ground Zero was a hunk of metal with a bunch of Bible pages fused to it. Someone had their Bible with them in the towers that fateful day. It must have been their "delight." That's what the psalmist calls God's Word in Psalm 119. In that chapter, he uses eight different terms for God's law. He calls it the Torah, the Word, the statutes, the commands, the decrees, the precepts, the promise, and the laws. Regardless of the term used, it was his delight. Do you cherish your Bible?

Day 92
THEY READ YOU

For the invisible things of him from the creation of the world are clearly seen, being understood by the things that are made, even his eternal power and Godhead; so that they are without excuse.

ROMANS 1:20 KJV

No one is excused.

The most cultured. The most primitive.

Everyone has the world to view. And it tells of God's power in great detail.

They also have you. They can see the witness in your life. You are a living testimony to His power to bring beauty to a human life.

Let others read a clear testimony today.

Day 93
LIFE FOREVERMORE

The LORD bestows his blessing,
even life forevermore.

PSALM 133:3 NIV

❧

Most of us have a vague idea about eternity, an
unknown realm beyond death, far off in the future.
But the psalmist is speaking in the present tense.
Eternal life starts now. The Hebrew word for this
life—*chayah*—has a breadth of meaning: to come
to life in a new way; to be restored to life after
being dead; to be healed; to be kept alive; to be
nourished; to recover from illness. And it's
all happening *right now*. We don't have
to wait until we die!

Day 94
WE ARE TO LIVE IN THE SPIRIT

But you are not controlled by your sinful nature.
You are controlled by the Spirit if you have
the Spirit of God living in you.

ROMANS 8:9 NLT

Sometimes I feel like I can't win. I agree with Paul's thoughts in Romans 7: I do what I don't want and don't do what I do want. I have to remember, though, that God has given me a new nature. It's my job to choose His nature over sin. When I do, I live where God wants me to—in His Spirit!

Day 95
WORTHLESS STUFF

Turn my eyes away from worthless things;
preserve my life according to your word.
PSALM 119:37 NIV

～

Women watch almost 166 hours of TV per month, 16 hours more than men. And yet, we often hear that homemakers do not have time to spend in God's Word. Truth is, the book of Malachi would take about eight minutes to read. We could consume the entire book of Genesis in about three hours and 45 minutes. Staying true to God's purposes requires time in His Book. Let's start turning our eyes away from the worthless stuff and spend time with our Savior.

Day 96
AN IMAGE OF HIS GLORY

But we all, with open face beholding as in a glass the glory of the Lord, are changed into the same image from glory to glory, even as by the Spirit of the Lord.

2 CORINTHIANS 3:18 KJV

You, with all your redeemed and surrendered beauty in Christ, are a witness to His glory.

All the fashion sense and fleeting trends of this world are suddenly very temporary when one has a glimpse of what it means to be loved by Him.

You are His image in the world.

Day 97
BEHIND THE SCENES

"When you do something for someone else, don't call attention to yourself. You've seen them in action, I'm sure—'playactors' I call them . . . acting compassionate as long as someone is watching, playing to the crowds. They get applause, true, but that's all they get. When you help someone out, don't think about how it looks. Just do it—quietly and unobtrusively. That is the way your God, who conceived you in love, working behind the scenes, helps you out.

MATTHEW 6:2–4 MSG

Here's how Jesus wants us to bless others—humbly, lovingly, with no focus on ourselves.

Day 98
WE OUTNUMBER THEM

---

*"When you go out to battle against your enemies
and see horses and chariots and people more
numerous than you, do not be afraid of them;
for the LORD your God, who brought you
up from the land of Egypt, is with you."*

DEUTERONOMY 20:1 AMP

~

Anyone who attempts to battle God will be sorely
disappointed. Remember what happened when
Elisha prayed for his servant's eyes to be opened?
He saw the hills were filled with horses and chariots
of fire. (See 2 Kings 6:17.) God's resources aren't
always seen, but they are there!

Day 99
CLEAN

Now ye are clean through the
word which I have spoken unto you.

JOHN 15:3 KJV

Every homemaker knows what it is to clean
something. So, we understand the principle that
Christ shed His blood to cleanse us from all
unrighteousness. In this verse, John uses a particular
word for *clean*. It is a Greek word from which we get
the term *catharsis*. This clean is more than the act
of just scrubbing; it is the process of getting relief
from something. So take a big breath as you
read His Word today, and relish the relief
from the shame associated with our sin.

Day 100
THE BRIDE PRICE

Knowing that you were not redeemed with corruptible things, like silver or gold, from your aimless conduct received by tradition from your fathers, but with the precious blood of Christ, as of a lamb without blemish and without spot.

1 PETER 1:18–19 NKJV

In ancient Israel (and in some countries today), a bride price must be paid to the family of the bride for the loss of their daughter, showing how valuable the woman is and how much the husband-to-be wants her.

Jesus paid the bride price for us with His own blood. It cost Him everything. We can tell by that how much we mean to Him.

Day 101
TRUE TREASURE

Do good. . .be rich in good works. . .be generous and ready to share, storing up. . .the treasure of a good foundation for the future, so that they may take hold of that which is life indeed.
1 TIMOTHY 6:18–19 NASB

༄

This verse explains what real wealth means, as well as the real purpose of wealth. Doing good to others is what makes us truly rich—and it's all meant to be shared! Giving builds the foundation we need not only for our future lives but for life itself. No other treasure lasts.

Day 102
BE SLOW TO ANGER

Be ye angry, and sin not.
EPHESIANS 4:26 KJV

～

"The sellers aren't going to pay for anything we listed from the inspection." I was shocked at Erik's comment. Negotiation and compromise are part of buying a home; their rude response made me want to give up on the home entirely—but I knew that acting out of anger would get us nowhere. Instead, I waited.

Nighttime came; my anger subsided. I knew the house was for my family; the anger was simply a detour from God's plan.

Don't act out of anger. Show love instead.

Day 103
YOUNG, UNTESTED

David the king addressed the congregation:
"My son Solomon was singled out and chosen
by God to do this. But he's young and untested."

1 CHRONICLES 29:1 MSG

David knew building the temple was a mammoth undertaking. He knew his son was young and inexperienced, but he also knew that God had chosen him for that assignment. Too often we focus on the training of an individual, their experience, their skill set, before we entrust them with a responsibility. God's plan is the opposite. He calls, then He equips. Regardless of your age, have you been given a task? Get it done.

Day 104
SHINE ON!

"Let your light so shine before men,
that they may see your good works
and glorify your Father in heaven."

MATTHEW 5:16 NKJV

God wants you to do good deeds in public. Not to be praised, but to be a neon sign pointing to Him.

As a woman who has dedicated her life to Him, you are His ambassador—His salesgirl so to speak. You are representing Him with every outfit you wear and every attitude you take.

So take care with your wardrobe, smile a little brighter, and shine on!

Day 105
GLIMPSES OF GOD

"You will seek Me and find Me when you search for Me with all your heart."

JEREMIAH 29:13 NASB

If God's always there, why can't we feel Him? If He's real, why doesn't He give us more proof of His presence? People have asked these questions for thousands of years. They're a part of human experience. But here's the answer: the life of faith wasn't meant to be easy. You have to give everything you have inside you—and only *then* will you begin to catch glimpses of God's presence, glimpses that will make you seek Him even harder.

Day 106
WE WAIT ON GOD

The horse is prepared for the day of battle,
but the victory belongs to the LORD.

PROVERBS 21:31 NLT

❧

As Christians, we plan our lives the way we think they should play out. The reality, though, is that we can prepare all day long, but in the end, the path to victory is given by the Lord. As the *Message* version of Proverbs 21:31 says, "Do your best, prepare for the worst—then trust GOD to bring victory."

Day 107
CARING FOR THE ELDERLY

---

*Any Christian woman who has widows
in her family is responsible for them.
They shouldn't be dumped on the church.*

1 TIMOTHY 5:16 MSG

Every year in the United States, 700,000 women
lose their husbands, and each of those gals will then
remain a widow for an average of fourteen years.
They all have needs, from simple things like a ride
to church to more significant issues like financial
assistance. Paul was establishing a priority for
women to help other women. It's a duty, not
an option. Is there someone in your family
who needs your help? Reach out today.

Day 108
SALTY, BRIGHT BEAUTY

"You are the salt of the earth; but if the salt loses its flavor, how shall it be seasoned? It is then good for nothing but to be thrown out and trampled underfoot by men. You are the light of the world. A city that is set on a hill cannot be hidden."

MATTHEW 5:13–14 NKJV

In the frenzy of fashion and the confusion of gender, your joyful celebration of the woman God appointed you to be is a lovely declaration of truth to the culture. Be salt. Be light. Spread the delightful savor of His splendor, and shine brightly on everyone near you.

Day 109
GOD'S LOVE SONGS

"The LORD your God is living among you. He is a mighty savior. He will take delight in you with gladness. With his love, he will calm all your fears. He will rejoice over you with joyful songs."

ZEPHANIAH 3:17 NLT

On the darkest, dreariest days—those days when just getting out of bed seems to take all your strength—remember: God is there with you, living in the midst of your life. You make Him happy, so happy that He's singing you love songs. Let His love calm and comfort your heart.

Day 110
FIGHT TOO MANY OPTIONS

He makes the whole body fit together perfectly.
As each part does its own special work, it helps
the other parts grow, so that the whole body
is healthy and growing and full of love.

EPHESIANS 4:16 NLT

Currently, new churches are popping up all over America. This trend is wonderful because it brings a small church atmosphere within a short driving distance of people everywhere. The problem for Christians is that it can create too many options. God wants us to connect to a specific local church and stay there. Pray that He leads you to the right church.

Day 111
GRAY HAIR

A gray head is a crown of glory.
PROVERBS 16:31 NASB

❧

Over the course of their lifetime, women may spend more than $20,000 coloring their gray hair. And that's if they do the job themselves. Clearly, the message that gray hair is a mark of distinction has been lost on many of us. In this verse, God is endorsing the wisdom to be gained through the ups and downs of everyday life. And there is a reward for those who do it well. Take a look in the mirror today and marvel at the crown of glory God has given you. Leave it gray!

Day 112
FOR YOUR OWN FAMILY

Her children stand and bless her;
so does her husband.
PROVERBS 31:28 TLB

You are beautiful for your family. Women were designed by God to be the beauty bearers and beauty creators in the home. Your beauty is not for you to consume for your own interests but for you to use in nurturing your husband and children. What can you do today to make their lives more beautiful?

Day 113
PILGRIMS

Blessed are those whose strength is in you,
whose hearts are set on pilgrimage. . . .
They go from strength to strength,
till each appears before God in Zion.

PSALM 84:5, 7 NIV

Pilgrims are people who go on long journeys, with God as their only destination. In a sense, our entire lives can be pilgrimages. Even though God is *always* with us, we perceive our life as a journey toward Him, with stopping places along the way. Again and again, God meets us anew—all the way to heaven.

Day 114
FABULOUS YOU

My frame was not hidden from You when I was being formed in secret [and] intricately and curiously wrought [as if embroidered with various colors] in the depths of the earth [a region of darkness and mystery].
PSALM 139:15 AMPC

You were made according to a pattern. No random fusion of DNA brought you into this world. Your parents may or may not have "planned" your creation, but God did. And while the little embryo that you once were was forming in that hidden place, God watched and waited until His masterpiece was ready to enter the outside world. And when the moment arrived, He knew you were beautiful. And you still are.

Day 115
HAPPINESS!

How blessed is the one whom
You choose and bring near to You.

PSALM 65:4 NASB

The Hebrew word used here means simply "happy." When God chooses us, He makes us happy. When He brings us near to Him, our hearts fill up with joy. We'll still have the ups and downs that everyone else has, of course. Sorrows will come, and we'll face days that challenge us. But when we look back at our lives as we enter eternity, we'll see clearly: we've been so blessed. God's given us so much to make us happy!

Day 116
YOU ARE AT PEACE

---

*Therefore, since we have been justified
by faith, we have peace with God
through our Lord Jesus Christ.*

ROMANS 5:1 ESV

～

Whether you're a soccer mom transporting kids everywhere, a businesswoman, a student juggling classes, or a combination of all three, peace may seem like the last thing possible to achieve. Yet the myriad of activities in your life do not need to upset your inner peace. Nothing you do—or don't do—will ever take away your standing of righteousness with God. Live with confidence that you have been made righteous in Him!

HE SAVED US

---

*He saved us, not because of righteous things
we had done, but because of his mercy.*

TITUS 3:5 NIV

∿

There is an interesting distinction between God's mercy (not receiving the condemnation we deserve) and His grace (receiving the blessings we do not deserve). Our best efforts are described in grotesque fashion in Isaiah 64:6. We deserve the wrath of God, but because of His mercy (literally, His compassion) we are saved. That reality gives enormous direction to our lives. As the old hymn says, "Saved, how I love to proclaim it, saved by the blood of the lamb, His child and forever I am!"

A BEAUTY OF BLESSING

*There are diversities of gifts, but the same Spirit.
There are differences of ministries, but the same
Lord. And there are diversities of activities,
but it is the same God who works all in all.
But the manifestation of the Spirit is
given to each one for the profit of all.*

1 CORINTHIANS 12:4–7 NKJV

❧

God gave you a gift in addition to your salvation.
You have been gifted with a spiritual ability, a
blessing to bring to the body of Christ. Look for
it. Discover the beautiful offering of service that
is uniquely yours to give.

Day 119
THE BLESSING OF TRUE IDENTITY

This is my beloved Son,
in whom I am well pleased.
MATTHEW 17:5 KJV

This is the blessing the Father gave to Jesus at the beginning of His ministry. It's a spoken affirmation of a reality that already existed. Through grace we, too, can claim this blessing as our own. When you feel down on yourself, when your self-concept feels beaten down to nothing, repeat this blessing to yourself. It affirms your true identity. Christ has made you part of His family, and now you are God's beloved child. He is pleased with you!

Day 120
YOU ARE CARED FOR

"And which of you by being anxious can add a single
hour to his span of life?. . . But if God so clothes
the grass of the field, which today is alive
and tomorrow is thrown into the oven,
will he not much more clothe you?"

MATTHEW 6:27, 30 ESV

Worry can feel productive; it's as though thinking
and rethinking through the situation will change it.
The truth though is that worry only changes your
stress level.

God cares for you and knows the situation you
are facing. Rest in Him; He'll take care of you.

Day 121
GOD HAS PLANS

"I have it all planned out—plans to take care of you, not abandon you, plans to give you the future you hope for."

JEREMIAH 29:11 MSG

In Hebrew, the phrase "the future you hope for" originally referred to a bright red cord like the one Rahab used in her window to save her family. Jeremiah uses that same symbolism to send Israel's deported leaders a message of hope and encouragement. Just as God promised Israel an expected end, He promises us a future that He controls. Watch for it.

Day 122
HE CRUNCHES THOSE NUMBERS

"And he knows the number of hairs on your head!"
LUKE 12:7 TLB

❧

Hair.

What that word represents to a woman is hard to fathom. It is deeply linked with her identity and her beauty. God designed it that way. Yet the inventory we have to work with is fluid, and God knows the exact number you are working with today. He sees strand #3984 dangling and about to fall to the floor. He is both the giver and the keeper of your hair. And you're beautiful to Him no matter the count today!

Day 123
SPIRITUALLY STRONG

I long to see you so that I may impart to you some spiritual gift to make you strong.

ROMANS 1:11 NIV

In this verse, Paul is talking about a particular kind of blessing: a spiritual gift. The Greek word is *charisma*, a grace-gift that empowers us to work on behalf of God's Kingdom. It's given to us freely; we don't have to do anything to earn it. We can't see this kind of blessing, but we can feel its power. It fills our lives with love, joy, and peace. We are spiritually strong. We have abundant life.

Day 124
YOU CAN REST

Be still before the LORD and wait patiently for him;
fret not yourself over the one who prospers in his
way, over the man who carries out evil devices!

PSALM 37:7 ESV

Waiting for your prayers to be answered is quite the test of patience. Usually, we want our prayers answered—now! But God doesn't work like that. He sees the big picture of our lives as well as that of everyone else in the world. Our job is to bring Him our prayers and cares, and then trust Him to answer.

Day 125
WE BELONG TO HIM

"Behold, all souls are Mine; the soul of the father as well as the soul of the son is Mine."

EZEKIEL 18:4 NASB

Nothing about us came by chance. Every woman has a distinct personality, exclusive fingerprints, and unique DNA markers. Where did all that uniqueness come from? We get the answer in Thornton Wilder's three-act play, *Our Town*. One of the characters in that play signs her address like this: "I live in Grover's Corner, New Hampshire, United States of America, Western Hemisphere, Planet Earth, Solar System, The Universe, and The Mind of God." We belong to Him!

Day 126
BEAUTIFULLY DISABLED

Who makes the dumb, or the deaf,
or the seeing, or the blind? Is it not I, the Lord?
EXODUS 4:11 AMPC

Cerebral palsy. Blindness. Deafness. Autism.

These are just a few of the disabilities that are part of the human story, perhaps your story. Part of your beauty.

We think of beauty only in classical, symmetrical, sculptured terms. But beauty can be painful, ill shapen, and random. Anything the Creator has allowed to pull you closer to Him is a thing of beauty.

Today, let your weaknesses become a reason to glory in His power.

Day 127
RELIABLE

We know and rely on the love
God has for us. God is love.

1 JOHN 4:16 NIV

~

When we talk about God's love, it's not just a pretty phrase or some lofty theological concept. The Greek word translated here as *know* implies firsthand experience. We know God's love because it touches us personally. The more we allow ourselves to experience His love, the more we will be able to trust that love. We can put our full weight on it, knowing that God will never jerk it out from under us. How could He, when His very nature is love?

Day 128
YOU CAN INTERCEDE

"I searched for someone to stand in the gap in the wall so I wouldn't have to destroy the land, but I found no one."

EZEKIEL 22:30 NLT

❧

Millions across this world need God. If you know Him, you can pray for God to reach them with His love. Now, you can't pray for everyone by name, but you can pray for other people as you are led. Random thoughts about friends, acquaintances, even celebrities, can be turned into prayers of intercession for their salvation. God desires for you to pray so He can impact their lives.

Day 129
YOU CAN INTERCEDE FOR YOUR NATION

"Make yourselves at home there and work for the country's welfare. Pray for Babylon's well-being. If things go well for Babylon, things will go well for you."

JEREMIAH 29:7 MSG

I'm learning how to include prayers for America in my daily living. Sometimes it's just by sending up "flare prayers"—that's what my middle school teacher called those quick prayers you utter as you think of someone. Other times, it's good to sit and pray more specific, lengthy prayers. Either way, keep your country in your prayers. When it prospers, you prosper.

INSTRUCTING OUR CHILDREN

Write these commandments that I've given you today on your hearts. Get them inside of you and then get them inside your children.

DEUTERONOMY 6:6–7 MSG

∽

Susanna Wesley was an English pastor's wife with nineteen children. Her sons John and Charles became notable Christian leaders of the Methodist movement. Through them, Susanna gained an amazing spiritual legacy. And she did it by taking personal time each week with each child. On Mondays she met with Molly, Tuesdays with Hetty, Wednesdays with Nancy, and so on. Her time with the children was intentional, steeped in scripture, and directed to Christ. How's your instruction time with your kids?

MADE FOR DILIGENCE

She watches over the ways of her household,
and does not eat the bread of idleness.
PROVERBS 31:27 NKJV

God thinks you are beautiful when you are fulfilling your role. Slothfulness is a blight on beauty; industriousness is a sign of inward character, and it is beautiful.

In the animal kingdom, the female species is often working to provide for her family's food. Many times, the female is the huntress. She rarely sits around idle.

While we are not identical to the animals, we are created to watch over our households. Today, be diligent. It's a sign of beauty.

Day 132
AT HOME IN THE LOVE OF JESUS

"Just as the Father has loved Me, I have also loved you; abide in My love."

JOHN 15:9 NASB

Jesus loves you just as much as His heavenly Father loves Him. Think about it. The Son of God, the Word that existed before the beginning of the world, loves you infinitely, unconditionally, with all His heart. What a blessing! The only thing He asks in return is that you make His love your home—that you seek out the place where your heart is close to His.

YOU CAN PRAY FOR YOURSELF

If you need wisdom, ask our generous God,
and he will give it to you. He will not
rebuke you for asking.

JAMES 1:5 NLT

Sometimes when I pray through the Pauline prayers found in Ephesians 1 and 3, Colossians 1, and Philippians 1, I don't include my name. Then one day, when I was stumped on how to respond to someone else, I realized that I needed prayer to know how to handle others.

When you're faced with a sticky situation, pray for the other person—and for you!

DO GOOD

As we have therefore opportunity, let us do good unto all men, especially unto them who are of the household of faith.

GALATIANS 6:10 KJV

～

Part of God's plan for our lives is the repeated action of doing useful, beneficial things for others. In this verse, Paul highlights the need to bless other Christians. Doing "good" in this sense means to provide a blessing. It could be a meal or some money or a place to live. But it is palpable. It's not just a promise to pray or a sweet sentiment. It's tangible. Let's consider what good we can do today.

Day 135
MOODS ARE NOT YOU

My tears have been my food day and night.
PSALM 42:3 AMPC

❧

Been there?

Moods are part of our humanity and, even more specifically, part of our femaleness. Maybe your mood is hormonally based, or maybe it is caused by your grief over a prodigal child, strained marriage, or broken friendship. Maybe you've recently moved or acquired a negative diagnosis or lost a job.

Remember that He is God of our moods also, even when we don't understand them. Today, He sees the beauty in you that passing moods cannot mar.

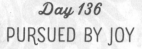

Day 136
PURSUED BY JOY

Gladness and joy will overtake them,
and sorrow and sighing will flee away.
ISAIAH 35:10 NIV

The Old Testament is filled with "joy words" that express different shades of meaning. In this verse, the Hebrew word *suws* contains within it the meanings of gladness, mirth, and rejoicing that we've already mentioned, but it has an added ingredient: "welcome." This is joy that runs after us with open arms. Even when we are deep in depression, wandering down dark and dreary paths, it catches up with us. Its presence—God's presence—chases away all our sadness.

Day 137
YOU CAN AGREE

"Again I say to you, if two of you agree on earth about anything they ask, it will be done for them by my Father in heaven."

MATTHEW 18:19 ESV

Did you know there is power available in agreement? When you and someone else gather together and pray, you unleash a greater power than when you pray on your own. So the next time someone asks you for prayer, don't wait until you're alone. Access a greater power and agree together with them in prayer then and there!

Day 138
HELP HER

I ask you to receive her in the Lord in a way worthy of his people and to give her any help she may need from you.

ROMANS 16:2 NIV

Paul is urging this church in Rome to meet the needs of a woman named Phoebe. He chooses a specific phrase to convey the concept—"give her any help she may need." Literally, he is asking them to stand by her, to place themselves at her disposal. The thought is to figure out exactly what she needs and provide it. There are people all around who need us to stand with them. Let's find some today.

Day 139
BEAUTY IN BEING KNOWN

For He knows the secrets of the heart.
PSALM 44:21 NKJV

Every woman has secrets.

Events that no one else witnessed.

Feelings that never surface on the outside.

Things known only to her. . .and to God.

We may secretly long for a romance of our own, a child, or a beautiful image. We may be hiding shame over an affair or an abortion. God, the Father, knows. And He wants us to trust Him with our secrets. He wants to show us the beauty of being known and loved and redeemed by His grace.

GOD IN ACTION

When the righteous see God in action, they'll laugh,
they'll sing, they'll laugh and sing for joy.
PSALM 68:3 MSG

❦

This Hebrew word for joy is *alats*, meaning "exults, rejoices in triumph." God is at work in our lives. His Spirit is moving and acting in amazing ways. What a blessing to know that the Creator of the world is working on our behalf, in a personal, intimate, ongoing way! How can we help but laugh and sing when we see Him triumph over the forces of darkness!

Day 141
YOU DON'T HAVE TO KNOW THE TIMING

God has made everything beautiful
for its own time.
ECCLESIASTES 3:11 NLT

❧

Waiting for your spouse—or for your children or grandchildren—can be a frustrating, slow process. That's why I felt slightly guilty that I got married four years before my best friend even met her spouse. Now I realize that the timing for both of us was perfect. She couldn't have married her honey any sooner, and I couldn't have married my man later. We blossomed in love when we trusted God with His perfect timing.

Day 142
A GOOD REPUTATION

Seest thou a man diligent in his business?
he shall stand before kings.
PROVERBS 22:29 KJV

❦

Most women appreciate having a good reputation. We would like to be noticed by our bosses. But how do we gain a good report? The Bible says that we must be "diligent." The original Hebrew word emphasizes a person's skill at their job. Before we "stand before kings," we have to patiently learn our jobs and then do them repetitively with excellence. Someone will notice.

Day 143
BEAUTIFUL DISCRETION

---

*As a ring of gold in a swine's snout, so is a
fair woman who is without discretion.*
PROVERBS 11:22 AMPC

If this is true (and the Bible always is), there are
many beautiful women in our world today who
present an image as awkward as a pig wearing
jewelry. The two don't go together.

Today, God wants you to know that you can have
beauty and discretion. You can possess beauty and
also know how to use it well. You can be good to
look at and not be bad for the conscience.

Get rid of the pig. Be beautifully discreet.

Day 144
HOMECOMING

*Well done, thou good and faithful servant. . .
enter thou into the joy of thy lord.*

MATTHEW 25:21 KJV

❧

The word Jesus uses is *chairo*. It implies cheerfulness, a calm delight that's also closely connected to grace, God's undeserved, freely given blessings. We need to be careful not to get turned around in our understanding: the faithful servant didn't *earn* the Lord's joy with his hard work. Joy was simply the home that lay at the end of the road, the natural endpoint to his lifetime of service—a place of blessing and grace waiting for him to come home.

YOU DON'T HAVE TO WORRY

Don't worry about anything; instead,
pray about everything. Tell God what you need,
and thank him for all he has done.

PHILIPPIANS 4:6 NLT

Have you ever noticed how your life stops when you are worried about something? Worry consumes your thoughts in an attempt to make the situation better.

But no amount of worry can alter circumstances. Only prayer can! Bring that situation to God and leave it with Him. You may need to mentally bring it to Him over and over, but do whatever it takes. Worry never works; prayer does.

Day 146
SATISFACTION IN OUR WORK

---

*A person can do nothing better than to eat
and drink and find satisfaction in their own toil.*

ECCLESIASTES 2:24 NIV

⤳

When God included work in His plan for our
lives, He never intended the endless stress that
accompanies much of our modern work world.
The term *satisfaction* in this verse implies rest or
the ability to lay something down and walk away.
When we work with the right attitude and for the
right reasons, it just feels good, and we can walk
away with a real sense of godly accomplishment.

Day 147
CHOICES ABOUT CHILDHOOD

---

*When I was a child, I talked like a child, I thought
like a child, I reasoned like a child; now that I
have become a man, I am done with childish
ways and have put them aside.*

1 CORINTHIANS 13:11 AMPC

Childhood experiences and events shape the adults
we are today. Some had an idyllic childhood; many
did not. Whatever your past, God will use it to
create beauty in you if you give Him permission
to filter it with His grace. Use your maturity to be
done with self-pity and make a choice to let
the healing begin.

Day 148
PEACE IN THE DESERT

The LORD's justice will dwell in the desert,
his righteousness live in the fertile field.
The fruit of that righteousness will be
peace. . .quietness and confidence forever.

ISAIAH 32:16–17 NIV

God's justice is simply the way He does things: fairly, without favoritism, ordering all things according to His own nature, creating peace and quiet confidence in our lives. The Hebrew word used here is *shalom*. It's more than freedom from conflict; it's also health and safety and completeness. It's ours not only in the midst of productive days like "fertile fields" but also in our empty "desert days."

Day 149
ABLE TO PARENT WELL

Train up a child in the way he should go:
and when he is old, he will not depart from it.

PROVERBS 22:6 KJV

I don't have a temper, so it amazes me how quickly I can raise my voice with my kids. Usually it's just to get my point across because I'm not sure they will hear me or respond any other way.

Children require a lot of patience, multiple times a day. When I catch myself raising my voice, I try to stop and remember I can parent well. Parenting patiently, as best as possible, is one way I show God's love to my kids.

Day 150
YOUR BUSINESS IS HIS BUSINESS

A just weight and balance are the LORD's:
all the weights of the bag are his work.
PROVERBS 16:11 KJV

In scripture, weights and other forms of measurement were the basis of commerce. A merchant's honesty was reflected by which weights he used. A wicked scale or a bag of deceptive weights (Micah 6:11) marked a seller as a cheat. And so it is today. Although not many of us are literally using weights, honesty still matters. Our word is a bond. How we conduct business reflects on our Savior. Our business is His business.

BLEMISHES BEYOND THE FACIAL VARIETY

Do not remember the sins of my youth, nor my transgressions; according to Your mercy remember me, for Your goodness' sake, O LORD.

PSALM 25:7 NKJV

Many of the events and decisions we regret occur in our teen years, our adolescence. With the hormonal, emotional, and physical upheaval that is the hallmark of puberty comes a wide-open opportunity for disastrous personal choice.

Maybe that's why the psalmist was anxious to have the Lord forget (redeem and cast away) his youthful indiscretions until only the beauty of those years was seen.

The beauty of a forgiven past can be yours today as well.

Day 152
SURRENDER

The mind governed by the Spirit
is life and peace.
ROMANS 8:6 NIV

All through the Bible, God promises peace to His people. And yet our lives and our hearts are all too often shaken by conflict and fear. How can we access the peace that God promises? How can we experience it as something more than a fleeting emotion? The apostle Paul gives us the answer here: we need to surrender our thoughts to the Holy Spirit. This isn't easy. It takes discipline. In another verse, Paul calls it "taking every thought captive." But it's well worth the effort!

Day 153

ABLE TO BRIGHTEN THE WORLD

Ye are the light of the world. A city that is set on an hill cannot be hid. Let your light so shine before men, that they may see your good works, and glorify your Father which is in heaven.

MATTHEW 5:14, 16 KJV

What happens when you turn a light on in a dark room? Darkness has no option; it must leave. When you shine your light for Jesus, darkness has no option as well. It must leave. Go shine your light to the world.

Day 154
SINCERITY

"My words come from an upright heart;
my lips sincerely speak what I know."

JOB 33:3 NIV

❧

When a mediocre chiseler makes a mistake in a statue, he might just smear some hot wax into the crack and pass it off as "good enough." The Latin term for not using wax is *sine cere*, from which we get the English word *sincere*. To speak sincerely is to be known as trustworthy. At home or in the office, let's make sure our words today are not just passed off with a "bit of wax." Let's be known as workers who have upright hearts.

Day 155
WHATEVER YOUR RÉSUMÉ

Whatever you do, do well, for in death,
where you are going, there is no working
or planning, or knowing, or understanding.
ECCLESIATES 9:10 TLB

Jobs come and go. We have a variety of them throughout our lifetimes. Some deliver a paycheck; others, like the incredible task of raising kids, do not.

Every job you've ever had becomes part of your beauty when it has passed through the purifying blood of Jesus in that moment of salvation. You can let go of the shame and hold only to the lessons of a life found in Him.

Your résumé: beautified!

Day 156
GOD KNOWS BEST

---

*This is what the LORD says—your Redeemer,
the Holy One of Israel: "I am the LORD your God,
who teaches you what is good for you and leads
you along the paths you should follow."*

ISAIAH 48:17 NLT

Sometimes we get in our heads that God likes to
say no. We hesitate to ask for His direction because
we're afraid He'll tell us we can't do something we
want to do. But that's not the way God works. His
guidance always is a yes to life, to health, to joy,
to blessing.

Day 157
ABLE TO RESCUE PRODIGALS

My dear friends, if you know people who have wandered off from God's truth, don't write them off. Go after them. Get them back and you will have rescued precious lives from destruction and prevented an epidemic of wandering away from God.

JAMES 5:19–20 MSG

Have you ever had that moment when you read a friend's Facebook update and think, *Really? I thought they knew Jesus.* I am slowly learning not to judge in that moment of realization. Instead, I should point them back to Jesus in prayer, in action, and—if God leads—in word.

Day 158
SALT

"Let me tell you why you are here. You're here to be salt-seasoning that brings out the God-flavors of this earth. If you lose your saltiness, how will people taste godliness?"
MATTHEW 5:13 MSG

Jesus knew salt is an essential seasoning for food from all cultures. It is important for food preservation and cooking. So He used salt as an illustration saying that it is our job to bring "God-flavoring" to the world. Without our active participation in service to others, no one gets to "taste and see that the LORD is good" (Psalm 34:8 KJV). So, out of the shaker and into the world!

Day 159
LOVELY MOTHERHOOD

He shall feed his flock like a shepherd:
he shall gather the lambs with his arm,
and carry them in his bosom, and shall
gently lead those that are with young.

ISAIAH 40:11 KJV

❧

God believes in motherhood. He created women, invented the process of procreation and birth, and sent His own Son into a womb on earth.

God affirms the emotions of motherhood; He delights in the beauty of motherhood. And He gently leads those who are tending young.

Today, He wants you to know that motherhood looks great on you.

Day 160
THE BLESSING OF INSOMNIA!

I will praise the L๐RD, who counsels me;
even at night my heart instructs me.

PSALM 16:7 NIV

༄

Do you ever lie awake, worrying? Do you sometimes
dread those long, sleepless hours when everything
looks darker than it does during the day? It doesn't
have to be that way. Instead, whenever we have
a bout of insomnia, we can use the time to open
our hearts to God. If we surrender each worry to
God, He can use this time to speak to our hearts.

Day 161
IMMERSE YOURSELF IN DISCIPLINE

Sin speaks a dead language that means nothing
to you; God speaks your mother tongue,
and you hang on every word.
ROMANS 6:10 MSG

Sometimes I feel like I don't have the ability to say no to my negative desires. Then one day I read what Paul wrote. I realized that I don't speak the language of sin anymore. When I accepted Christ into my life, I accepted a new standard of living—and the ability of God to help me live that way. He knows how to help me live disciplined before Him.

Day 162
SERVE ONE ANOTHER

By love serve one another.

GALATIANS 5:13 KJV

ও৺

In the context of teaching on spiritual freedom, Paul makes the grand statement that encapsulates all of the Christian life: serve one another. And he uses a term for *serve* that directly reflects the life of a slave. It literally means "act like a slave to everyone around you." Volunteer to put their needs above your own. Do what needs to be done, and do it selflessly. It is a tough command that can't be ignored if we want to follow God's plan for our lives.

Day 163
HOLY BEAUTY

So that he could give her to himself as a glorious Church without a single spot or wrinkle or any other blemish, being holy and without a single fault.
EPHESIANS 5:27 TLB

Christ died to make the Church, His bride, holy. He did for her what she could not do herself.

If you have given your heart to Him, you are more than part of the collective bride of Christ; you are an individual, beloved by Him, beautified through His sacrifice on the cross.

No price was too high for Him to ensure your holy beauty.

Day 164
BLESSED BY WORSHIP

"Worship the LORD your God, and his blessing will be on your food and water. I will take away sickness from among you."

EXODUS 23:25 NIV

❧

The word translated *worship* in this verse actually means "serve" or "work for," in the way that a farmer works the land or an employee works for her employer. It means serving God with our actions—and with our thoughts. When we do, He has promised to bless the food we eat and the water we drink. He will bless our bodies, and He will heal our hearts.

IMMERSE YOURSELF IN RADICAL THINKING

"To you who are ready for the truth, I say this: Love your enemies. Let them bring out the best in you, not the worst. . . . Live generously."
LUKE 6:27–28, 30 MSG

"They bring out the worst in me." Although this phrase is common, when you're following Christ, it should not describe you. In fact, God wants the opposite to happen. Every time you see someone you're at odds with, let them bring out your best. Let your knowledge of God's love for them propel you to love them generously.

DEALING WITH DEPRESSION

"And if you give yourself to the hungry and satisfy the desire of the afflicted, then your light will rise in darkness and your gloom will become like midday."

ISAIAH 58:10 NASB

The prophet Isaiah seemed to understand that one of the best ways to deal with depression is to get active and involve yourself in someone else's life. The Hebrew word for *gloom* means a kind of darkness. It makes life obscure. But when we feed the hungry or help the sick, our world brightens and our energy level soars. Reaching out in service turns on the light for all of us.

Day 167
KEPT LIKE A PRINCESS

*You, who are kept by the power
of God through faith for salvation.*
1 PETER 1:4–5 NKJV

~

A trend in decorating refers to the main room in a house as the "keeping room." The term dates back to colonial times, referring to a large, multiuse room attached to the kitchen area.

God has you in a "keeping room." If you belong to Him, you are surrounded by His power and covered from anything outside of His will for you. He has you in the palm of His hand. Like a princess protected by a knight, you are safe.

Day 168
FIRST THINGS FIRST

Those who seek the LORD lack no good thing.

PSALM 34:10 NIV

The psalmist is reminding us again of what our priorities should be. We don't need to worry about material blessings. We don't need to focus our thoughts on them. Instead, we need to turn all our attention to the Lord. When we do, He will take care of our material needs. He will make sure we don't lack anything. When He is our priority, we can leave everything else up to Him.

Day 169
IMMERSE YOURSELF IN SINGING

Sing to the LORD; praise his name.
Each day proclaim the good news that he saves.

PSALM 96:2 NLT

⌇

Music impacts us. That's why singing quickly uplifts your spirits. More than once, I've been walking down the street pondering my problems and a song will come to my heart. The song reminds me of exactly what I need in that moment, whether it's a reminder that God is good or everything will work out. Since songs provide the background for your life, why not make sure that background will strengthen you in your faith?

Day 170
IN ORDER TO SERVE, WE NEED TO "SEE"

*"For God sees not as man sees, for man
looks at the outward appearance,
but the LORD looks at the heart."*

1 SAMUEL 16:7 NASB

༄

As if women can't be catty enough on their own, there are now apps on our phones that can rate the attractiveness of women around us. These apps scan a person's face and, using optimal measurements, instantly rate that person's attractiveness. The developers claim it's all in good fun, but it just sounds like another way to evaluate people on the basis of their looks. Let's stop that and learn to see others as God sees them.

Day 171
HOLY ADRENALINE

As you live this new life, we pray that you will
be strengthened from God's boundless resources,
so that you will find yourselves able to
pass through any experience and
endure it with courage.

COLOSSIANS 1:11 PHILLIPS

God living inside us through His Holy Spirit gives us power, a kind of holy adrenaline. You may be a single woman. You may have lost a spouse. You may be surrounded by children and their needs. You may be in a difficult marriage. Whatever the place, God has promised you the resources through His grace to live there.

Day 172
THE BLESSING STOREHOUSE

The LORD will open the heavens, the storehouse
of his bounty, to send rain on your land in season
and to bless all the work of your hands.

DEUTERONOMY 28:12 NIV

Most of us go to work every day, in one form or
another. We work in offices, schools, factories, and
hospitals; in yards and homes; on farms, boats, and
roadways. Some of us like our work. Some of us
are doing the work only for the paycheck. Either
way, God has promised to reach into the enormous
warehouse where He keeps His blessings—and rain
them down on our jobs.

Day 173
HE IS OMNISCIENT

---

*And there came a voice to him, Rise, Peter; kill,
and eat. But Peter said, Not so, Lord; for I have
never eaten any thing that is common or unclean.
And the voice spake unto him again the
second time, What God hath cleansed,
that call not thou common.*

ACTS 10:13–15 KJV

❧

God directed Peter to do something different from
what was religiously acceptable. If God asks you to
do something you don't understand, obey anyway.
Just as Peter did, you'll get to live out your
part of God's greater plan on this earth.

Day 174
HE IS PREPARING A PLACE FOR US

*"If I go and prepare a place for you, I will
come again and receive you to Myself,
that where I am, there you may be also."*

JOHN 14:3 NASB

When a king in the Ancient Near East traveled
toward home, special servants were dispatched in
order to get things ready. The lodging was prepped,
meals were made, and hospitality was arranged.
They *prepared* for the arrival of someone important.
John uses this same term to convince us that Christ
has gone before us to prepare our eternal home.
And He is coming back for us. Bank on it.

Day 175
SAY NO TO POUTING

Never act from motives of rivalry or personal
vanity, but in humility think more of each
other than you do of yourselves.

PHILIPPIANS 2:3 PHILLIPS

You know the story of the pampered, pouty
princess, right?

Well, maybe Disney never made a movie about
her, but there is certainly the temptation to take on
that persona. Beauty that is turned inward sours.
It turns to ugliness.

Today, God wants you to know that your beauty
is meant to be selfless. He gave His grace
to you; you are to share it with others.

Day 176
GOD'S METAPHORS

"God, who helps you. . .who blesses you with blessings of the skies above, blessings of the deep springs below."
GENESIS 49:25 NIV

The next time you look up at a blue, blue sky, remember that it is an expression of God's blessing. When you feel the sun on your face or moonlight pours through your window, think of God's light shining in your heart. When you see water spilling clear and bright out of the earth, remember that Jesus is a well of living water springing up within you.

Day 177
HE IS OUR SHELTER

The LORD is my rock, my fortress, and my savior;
my God is my rock, in whom I find protection.
He is my shield, the power that saves
me, and my place of safety.

PSALM 18:2 NLT

Have you ever looked outside the window to realize it was raining hard—and you had no idea because you were sheltered inside your house or office? When we're in God's family, He does that for us. He protects us from getting wet in the rains of life, even when we are unaware He's there. Isn't that awesome?

Day 178
FULL WARRANTY

*God's gifts and God's call are under full
warranty—never canceled, never rescinded.*

ROMANS 11:29 MSG

There is nothing worse than trying to return
something to a store that does not want to honor
its warranties. God is not like that. What He says
stands. His offer of salvation through the sacrifice
of His Son will never be rescinded. His purposeful
provision of eternal life for His kids will never be
cancelled. We can count on it. Rest in it today.

Day 179
EMPOWERED TO LOVE

All the special gifts and powers from God will someday come to an end, but love goes on forever.

1 CORINTHIANS 13:8 TLB

Love is perhaps the Christian virtue most discussed today, but it is not primarily an emotion; it is an action.

Love stems from a choice to seek the good of another, to be kind, show mercy, and give expecting nothing in return.

We as women who know Christ are to exemplify love in our daily lives. We can do this practically by affirming others. Give a compliment to someone today. That's beautifully loving.

Day 180
NATURE'S BOUNTY

O LORD, how manifold are thy works!
in wisdom hast thou made them all:
the earth is full of thy riches.
PSALM 104:24 KJV

∾

The earth brims over with God's abundance: countless fish in the sea, thousands of species of flowers and butterflies and feathered creatures; trillions of tiny creatures too small for us to see; sunset after sunset and sunrise after sunrise; ocean and desert, forest and rivers. Everywhere we turn, we see beauty that tells us of the bountiful blessings of our Lord.

Day 181
HE IS GLORIOUS

We saw it with our own eyes: Jesus resplendent with light from God the Father as the voice of Majestic Glory spoke: "This is my Son, marked by my love, focus of all my delight." We were there on the holy mountain with him. We heard the voice out of heaven with our very own ears.

2 PETER 1:16–18 MSG

Imagine that moment Jesus was "resplendent with light." It was an out-of-the-ordinary display of God's glory that showed the world that the God we serve is beautiful, glorious, and beyond our comprehension. He deserves our praise.

Day 182
THIS IS MY STORY

"Return home and tell how much
God has done for you."

LUKE 8:39 NIV

After Jesus healed him, the demon-possessed man began to beg for the opportunity to travel with the Lord and His disciples. He wanted to be part of the spiritual gang, but Jesus had a more important job for him. He had a personal story to tell, and it needed to be shared. Each of us has a unique platform from which to tell our own story. Our eternal destiny is secure; let's share the news.

Day 183
AMAZING THOUGHTS

"But there is a spirit in man, and the breath
of the Almighty gives him understanding."
JOB 32:8 NKJV

✿

You are beautiful from the inside out.

You were designed to radiate beauty from your very core. Often, we feel our opinions and perspective aren't significant. You may express your view and others keep right on talking. You may tell a joke and not get laughter. You may have a great idea that is ignored. But God listens to every nuance of your mind and is delighted with the person He created. To Him, you are brilliant and interesting.

Day 184
SPOKEN

*"Come, you who are blessed by my Father,
inherit the Kingdom prepared for you
from the creation of the world."*

MATTHEW 25:34 NLT

The Greek word translated *blessed* in the
New Testament adds another meaning to our
understanding. In this verse, the word Jesus uses
means "to speak well of, to say words that give or
create something good." Speaking is important in
the Bible. In Genesis, God spoke the world into
being. Jesus is the Word. And your name is on
God's lips. He has spoken your very self into being.
You are a child of the Kingdom!

Day 185
YOU ARE ABLE

"Get out of here, Satan," Jesus told him.
*"For the Scriptures say, 'You must worship
the LORD your God and serve only him.'"*
Then the devil went away.

MATTHEW 4:10–11 NLT

❧

I can't comprehend the thoughts running through
Jesus' head on the fortieth day of his fast. He was
ravenous and beyond exhausted, yet He still had the
ability to say no to the enemy, three times in a row.

If Jesus could do it then, we can do it now.
We can say no to the enemy. We are able
because He first did.

Day 186
WE HAVE GREAT DIGNITY

For as the heavens are higher than the earth,
so are my ways higher than your ways,
and my thoughts than your thoughts.

ISAIAH 55:9 KJV

⁓

God's "ways" (operational principles) are "higher" than ours. The Hebrew term means "to be exalted," and it refers to people or things of high or great dignity. God has a plan for us, and in it we have great worth. Left to our own devices, we will muddle through life making marginal spiritual progress. But once we realize that His way is superior, we have value and much dignity. Great thought to start the day with!

NOT FOUND ON PINTEREST

"And to one he gave five talents, to another two, and to another one, to each according to his own ability."

MATTHEW 25:15 NKJV

✑

One of a kind. That's you. With one-of-a-kind creativily.

Many women say, "I'm not creative." Not true.

Of course, it's easy to see why we would feel that way with Pinterest boards that show us all the wonderful things we could do in our spare time, and then with our friends' Facebook posts that show us "everyone else" actually doing them!

But you have unique creativity given from God.

Believe that today!

THE SECRET OF MATERIAL BLESSINGS

Be harmonious. . .kindhearted, and humble in spirit;
not returning evil for evil or insult for insult,
but giving a blessing instead; for you were
called for the very purpose that
you might inherit a blessing.

1 PETER 3:8–9 NASB

೬ಞ

These verses contain two meanings of the Greek word for *blessing*: first, speaking well of others (this is one way we bless others, by affirming them with our words, rather than gossiping, insulting, boasting, or quarreling), and second (the consequence of the first), tangible good things in our ordinary lives.

YOU ARE INFLUENTIAL

Death and life are in the power of the tongue:
and they that love it shall eat the fruit thereof.
PROVERBS 18:21 KJV

The direction of my life was deeply impacted by my tenth-grade teacher's verbal encouragement—words she probably doesn't remember speaking at all. It's a great reminder that our influence extends further than we realize—and much of that influence starts in our mouths. Our words have great impact. Use this influence wisely.

Day 190
GUIDED BY HIS EYE

I will instruct thee and teach thee in the way which
thou shalt go: I will guide thee with mine eye.
PSALM 32:8 KJV

❧

As children, we all knew what it was like to be
directed by our parents via one of those "looks."
In a similar way, the psalmist is letting us know that
God is actively guiding our lives and He is doing so
with His eyes. Literally, it means that He is giving
us silent counsel or advice. He is accomplishing His
plans, guiding us through the circumstances of life,
and His plans will never fail. Check out His eyes!

Day 191
BEAUTIFUL PLAN

But from the beginning of the creation
God made them male and female.

MARK 10:6 KJV

෴

The idea of two distinct genders and their relationship to each other is a beautiful one. It was God's.

He designed male and female to reflect His glorious image in their complementary, covenantal relationship.

You are a specific example of this magnificent plan.

Today, embrace your beautiful femininity and express it graciously and wholesomely. Be a model of God's greatness.

Day 192
HEARTS FULL OF LOVE

God's love has been poured out into our
hearts through the Holy Spirit.
ROMANS 5:5 NIV

～

God's love touches our entire lives. Even better,
He pours His love into our very being. We are like
a cup that God never stops filling up with His love.
Love is a constant stream flowing into us until that
love runs over and spills out to others. Because we
have been blessed with God's unfailing love, we
can pass that blessing on to others.

Day 193
YOU CAN COME BOLDLY

So let us come boldly to the throne of our gracious God.

HEBREWS 4:16 NLT

❧

When I was younger, I was greatly impacted by Brother Jesse Duplantis's morning routine. He'd wake and say, "Hello, God." He'd hear, "Hi, Jesse!"

My thoughts raced. God doesn't play favorites. If he can be that close to God, I can too. So that's what I do—I approach God boldly. He is my Lord, and He's also my friend.

He loves you as He loves me and Jesse. Take down religious barriers, and talk to Him as a friend.

Day 194
CHANGED

And we all, who with unveiled
faces contemplate the Lord's glory,
are being transformed into his image.
2 CORINTHIANS 3:18 NIV

❧

"Are being transformed": this is the Greek word *metamorphosis*. It's a change of condition. Not because of anything we have done, but by His grace we are being formed into His image. We have great worth because we are slowly becoming like Him. Think butterfly. The invisible process of spiritual transformation is at work. Changed for a purpose!

MORE THAN SKIN DEEP

So it was, when Abram came into Egypt,
that the Egyptians saw the woman,
that she was very beautiful.
GENESIS 12:14 NKJV

༄

We know Sarah was beautiful. But she was a woman
who was beautiful while living in a desert land,
exposed to harsh sun, blowing winds, and a nomadic
lifestyle. And skin keeps no secrets.

Today, God says you are beautiful despite what
your skin says to others. He sees the beauty that
goes beyond "skin deep." He sees the spirit,
which is preserved and made forever
young by His grace.

GOD'S HOUSE OF JOY

Strength and joy are in his dwelling place.
1 CHRONICLES 16:27 NIV

When we feel as though we're too weak to accomplish anything, we often feel blue and depressed. Our self-concepts suffer. We measure ourselves against others around us and come up lacking. But it doesn't have to be that way. When we stop focusing on our own lack and instead turn our eyes to God, He welcomes us with open arms into His house—a place where joy and strength go hand in hand.

Day 197
YOU CAN BE PERSISTENT

[Elijah] cast himself down upon the earth, and put his face between his knees, and said to his servant, Go up now, look toward the sea. And he went up, and looked, and said, There is nothing. And he said, Go again seven times. And it came to pass at the seventh time, that he said, Behold, there ariseth a little cloud out of the sea, like a man's hand.

1 KINGS 18:42–44 KJV

Circumstances change when we are bold enough to be persistent in our prayers. Elijah lived this truth; so can we.

Day 198
CALLED TO A HOLY LIFE

He has saved us and called us to a holy life.
2 TIMOTHY 1:9 NIV

❧

God has saved us by His grace and for His own purposes. Once saved, we are called to a different kind of life. We no longer control our activities or future. To be holy does not convey moral perfection. A holy life is one set aside for specific reasons. It is to be consecrated for a virtuous cause. We no longer call the shots; He directs our lives toward a specific service.

Day 199
CREATED FOR CREATIVITY

She makes linen garments and sells them,
and supplies sashes for the merchants.
PROVERBS 31:24 NKJV

Having a home business is commended in the Bible. The Proverbs 31 woman was very definitely involved in the keeping and nurturing of her home, but she also had some business ventures going. One of them was creating beautiful items of clothing to sell to the merchants for their shops.

Using your God-given talents as an investment or to help meet the needs of your family can be a blessing. Beauty is found in creatively using your gifts for the good.

Day 200
ABUNDANT GOODNESS

Be glad in the L𝑜𝑅𝐷 and rejoice,
you righteous ones; and shout for joy,
all you who are upright in heart.

PSALM 32:11 NASB

～

We often think of the Old Testament as being a bit gloomier than the New Testament—but look at all the verses that promise joy! Here our gladness is connected with the great bounty of blessings God has given to us. I'm reminded of a short verse by Robert Louis Stevenson: "The world is so full of a number of things, I'm sure we should all be as happy as kings." If we open our eyes, we'll see that God has filled our lives with abundant goodness.

Day 201
YOU CAN GIVE THANKS

---

*Always giving thanks to God the Father for all
things, in the name of our Lord Jesus Christ.*
EPHESIANS 5:20 AMP

One of my favorite moments when something
good has happened is the moment I remember
to say, "Thanks!" to the Lord. In that moment, I am
reminded of God's faithfulness. I try to keep that
habit going even when bad things happen—because
we always have something we can be thankful for.

Day 202
SERVING OUR FAMILIES

---

*First thing in the morning, she dresses for work,
rolls up her sleeves, eager to get started.*

PROVERBS 31:15 MSG

❧

We often joke that a mother's work is never done,
and it's true. There is an endless pile of laundry,
a recurring clamor for meals, and so on it goes.
There is always something to be accomplished.
But it is not the long list of tasks that's laudable;
it's Mom's attitude that counts. Part of God's plan
for all of us is to care for our families and to do so
with an enthusiastic mind-set. Are you eager for
the demands of today?

CRAVINGS BEAUTIFIED

Delight yourself also in the Lord, and He will give you the desires and secret petitions of your heart.

PSALM 37:4 AMPC

❧

What do you crave? Besides chocolate. Or a new pair of shoes.

All of us have longings—things that are often too personal to express.

Our Father in heaven tells us to bring our desires to Him. But first, we are to delight ourselves in Him, find in Him our highest joy. Then our cravings will be framed by our desire for His will in us, and the beauty of that is beyond compare.

Day 204
THE BRIDEGROOM

As a young man marries a young woman, so will your Builder marry you; as a bridegroom rejoices over his bride, so will your God rejoice over you.

ISAIAH 62:5 NIV

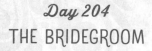

Imagine you're at a wedding. Now picture the way the groom looks at the bride as she walks down the aisle toward him. Can you see his look of total love and joy? His face tells everyone there how much he loves this woman, how glad he is to join his life with hers. That's how God loves you. You fill His heart with joy. He loves you so much that He wants to give Himself totally to you.

Day 205
ABLE TO SHARE YOUR STORY

We will not hide these truths from our children;
we will tell the next generation about the
glorious deeds of the LORD, about his
power and his mighty wonders.

PSALM 78:4 NLT

❧

Our friend Pastor Nate Ruch once said, "The stories
your kids are hearing become their faith." It's true.
My faith has been impacted greatly by watching
people close to me live their faith. We should be
open with our kids about what God is doing in our
hearts. As Pastor Nate concluded, let people
hear our story and not just our doctrine.

Day 206
TOUCH THEM

And they were bringing children to Him
so that He might touch them.
MARK 10:13 NASB

༄

Women understand the power of a touch. When we are physically touched in kindness, our blood pressure goes down, endorphins are released, and we just plain feel good. Two-handed handshakes are better than one. A tousle of the hair means something. A pat on the back is much more than just an expression; it is an affirmation of a job well done. A hand on the shoulder is reassuring. Jesus touched people; so should we.

TRANSITIONS FOR A PURPOSE

To every thing there is a season,
and a time to every purpose under the heaven.

ECCLESIASTES 3:1 KJV

"Nothing endures but change," says the old adage. And it does seem true. Nothing lasts forever. Clothes wear out, neighborhoods deteriorate, bodies age, children grow up, spouses die—the earth and people are ever changing. This is the way of life on earth.

Today, God wants you to see that He is using these changing tides to give you more beauty, to shape you after His plan.

Day 208
THE SPIRITUAL BLESSING OF PEACE

"Peace I leave with you; My peace I give to you. . . . Do not let your heart be troubled, nor. . .fearful."

JOHN 14:27 NASB

❧

Jesus shares with us His own peace. Imagine that! We have access to the same peace of mind and heart He experienced during His life on earth. It's the legacy He left us, His going-away gift when He went back to His Father. "Don't let yourself be troubled," He tells us, indicating that we have a choice in the matter. All we have to do is accept this spiritual blessing He's shared with us.

ABLE TO FIND THEM

*"But I say, wake up and look around.
The fields are already ripe for harvest."*
JOHN 4:35 NLT

One day, we spent three hours hunting for the TV remote. We didn't know where to look, so we just did what we know to do: clean, straighten, and go about our daily lives until it appeared.

Sometimes our Christian lives imitate this game of hide-and-seek. We don't know where to find unsaved people—but if we will keep our eyes open, God will bring them into our lives so we can minister to them!

Day 210
ORGANIZATION

Let all things be done decently and in order.
1 CORINTHIANS 14:40 KJV

Although the immediate context for this verse is an organized church service, the principle applies to all endeavors. Much of our purpose in life involves our work. Work that is pleasing to the Lord is "done decently" or with decorum. The original language stipulates that our work should be fashioned well. And it is accomplished in good "order," meaning it is well regulated and without confusion. No one wants to work in an environment of chaos. Have you considered that being organized is a spiritual hallmark too?

Day 211
THE DAY OF YOU

A good name is better than precious perfume,
and the day of death better than
the day of one's birth.
ECCLESIASTES 7:1 AMPC

～

Birthdays remind us that life is a moving line, a continuum. We aren't standing still here. Birthdays tell us that we have passed through another yearly cycle of seasons—spring, summer, winter, and fall. Birthdays are a one-day celebration that is determined by the other 364. Birthdays remind us that living takes awhile to do.

And each day crossed off the calendar makes us just a little more beautiful in God.

Day 212
ANOINTED WITH JOY

Your God has anointed you,
pouring out the oil of joy.
HEBREWS 1:9 NLT

～

We find more promises of joy in the New Testament. The Greek word used here is *agalliao*, which contains within it the sense of both joyful welcome and exceeding gladness. It brings to mind the image of my mother's expression when I returned home for a Christmas gathering. As I came through the door, her face lit with such welcome as she hurried to give me whatever she could to make me happy. That's the sort of loving joy God pours over us!

Day 213
IMMERSE YOURSELF IN GOD'S WORD

I have hidden your word in my heart,
that I might not sin against you.
PSALM 119:11 NLT

Enduring through difficulty can feel impossible, but it isn't. Read, study, or memorize God's Word, and give yourself ammunition to make it through difficult times.

When you are alone, the Holy Spirit can remind you of Hebrews 13:5. When you are scared, you'll remember Psalm 23. When you need healing, Isaiah 53:4-5 will come to mind. The Word of God is filled with power. It will strengthen you when you need it the most.

Day 214
COMMITTING OUR WORK TO GOD

Commit thy works unto the LORD,
and thy thoughts shall be established.
PROVERBS 16:3 KJV

The root idea of the Hebrew word for *commit* means "to roll." When someone's work was "rolled" to God, it was committed or entrusted to Him. It is a way to say, "Lord, here are my efforts for today. I give them to You to bless." And when we do that, our minds are settled; our thoughts are focused. We are working out a part of His plan, and it feels good.

Day 215
MADE TO HOLD HIS GLORY

Being filled with the fruits of righteousness,
which are by Jesus Christ, unto the
glory and praise of God.

PHILIPPIANS 1:11 KJV

God does not want you to be an empty beauty.
He takes no delight in a beautiful but barren
container. You were made to hold His righteousness
and His glory. Sin defiled us and made us unfit for
Him. But through the redemption offered in Christ,
it is now possible for us to have His very life within
us. That is the ultimate beauty treatment.
He holds it out to you.

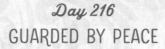

Day 216
GUARDED BY PEACE

Then you will experience God's peace,
which exceeds anything we can understand.
His peace will guard your hearts and
minds as you live in Christ Jesus.
PHILIPPIANS 4:7 NLT

We all crave peace. We long for that quiet sense that all is as it should be. It seems like too much to ask, though. After all, everyone has their share of troubles. But God's peace is deeper, wider, and greater than any peace we can imagine. We can't understand it—but we can experience it. It will guard our thoughts and emotions, even in the middle of heartache and trouble.

IMMERSE YOURSELF IN GOOD THINKING

Fix your thoughts on what is true, and honorable, and right, and pure, and lovely, and admirable. Think about things that are excellent and worthy of praise.

PHILIPPIANS 4:8 NLT

Our thoughts indicate the direction our life will take. That's why I am continually attempting to train my mind to think beneficial thoughts. When I start to get angry, I count in my head. When I'm doing something boring, I focus on the finish line.

I encourage you to ask the Lord to help you keep your mind and heart on Him.

Day 218
THROW A PARTY

Serve the Lord with gladness.
PSALM 100:2 KJV

❧

We serve the Lord when we serve others. The psalmist set the tone for that service when he wrote this song. That word *gladness* in Hebrew reflects the activities associated with the feast days of Israel or a wedding celebration. If we were translating it today, we might say something like: "Let's throw a party and serve the Lord!" Truth is, serving our neighbors or coworkers shouldn't be a chore. Done with the right attitude, it's a celebration!

JUSTIFIED AND PEACEFUL

Therefore being justified by faith, we have peace with God through our Lord Jesus Christ.

ROMANS 5:1 KJV

❧

In itself, beauty does not bring peace. It is a source of stress and envy, of endless searching. There is always a new diet to try or fitness program to embrace. There is no end to the choices in cosmetics, hair color and skin products, enhancement surgeries and face-lifts. The carousel never stops.

We must approach our God-given beauty with the knowledge that it is being justified by faith. That gives us peace, and the carousel ride doesn't make us dizzy anymore.

Day 220
SPIRITUAL EARS

Whether you turn to the right or to the left,
your ears will hear a voice behind you,
saying, "This is the way; walk in it."

ISAIAH 30:21 NIV

Can you imagine how wonderful it would be if we could actually hear God's voice in our ears, whispering, "Go this way. Go that way. Now go *this* way." Maybe we depend too much on our five senses, though. We need to practice using our spiritual senses. If we want to hear God's voice, we need to listen with the ears of our spirits.

HE IS OUR HEALER

By [Jesus'] stripes ye were healed.
1 PETER 2:24 KJV

∽

The summer after my three-year-old had been born, I went to see the doctor about recurring shooting pain in my wrists. I was shocked when the doctor determined the solution was surgery. I walked away resolved to pray about the advice before making a decision.

Sure enough, the Great Physician provided an answer. In the following months, the pain stopped, and I haven't had any for years.

God doesn't favor one person over another. If He can heal me, He can heal you too.

THE FOLKS WITH CARDBOARD SIGNS

"You shall not harden your heart, nor close your hand from your poor brother; but you shall freely open your hand to him."

DEUTERONOMY 15:7–8 NASB

～

We have all driven by the folks on the side of the road holding up cardboard signs. Too often we instinctively start an analysis of whether they really need our help. We check out their shoes, look for labels on their jeans, anything that can disqualify them from asking for some money. But take another look at Moses' instruction: Do not "harden your heart." Do not "close your hand." Maybe we need a different mind-set.

DIGITS BY DESIGN

For You did form my inward parts;
You did knit me together in my mother's womb.
PSALM 139:13 AMPC

❧

I wonder how many of us actually like our fingers and toes.

Personally, I never have cared for mine. I wanted slender, tapered fingers and toes that decreased gradually in length. Alas, it was not to be. But still, our Creator has designed us to fulfill His plan, and He has given us the fingers and toes to accomplish it.

Today, marvel at the function of your digits, no matter their shape.

Day 224
CONSECRATED

*The cup of blessing which we bless, is it not
the communion of the blood of Christ?*

1 CORINTHIANS 10:16 KJV

The Greek word used here means "consecration,"
in other words, to commit something totally to God.
This adds another element to our understanding of
blessing: something that is blessed is completely
surrendered to God. We commune in our hearts with
Christ—we share intimately with Him His absolute
self-giving on the cross—and this consecrates us.
Our hearts are God's. We have drunk from Christ's
cup of sacrifice and blessing.

Day 225
UNFADING BEAUTY

*Don't be concerned about the outward beauty of
fancy hairstyles, expensive jewelry, or beautiful
clothes. You should clothe yourselves instead with
the beauty that comes from within, the unfading
beauty of a gentle and quiet spirit,
which is so precious to God.*

1 PETER 3:3–4 NLT

Something blossoms in women when we get our
hair done and put on a fancy dress. We love to
look beautiful.

The greatest beauty, though, doesn't come with
extra mascara or hairspray. It comes from
within. Wear your smile, and love the
Lord; you'll shine from the inside out.

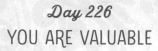

Day 226
YOU ARE VALUABLE

---

*"So do not fear; you are more
valuable than many sparrows."*
MATTHEW 10:31 NASB

❧

A sparrow is a small brown or gray bird that feeds on seeds and tiny insects and is found in great numbers around Israel. They had little value, but Jesus said that one of them could not fall to the ground without the heavenly Father knowing about it. And then He went on to say that we are "more valuable" than those sparrows. In Greek that phrase carries the idea of superior worth. What is worth more than the constant attention of God Almighty? Wow, we are valuable!

TEMPERED TRAITS

*"I knew you before you were formed within
your mother's womb; before you were born
I sanctified you and appointed you
as my spokesman to the world."*

JEREMIAH 1:5 TLB

To what has God appointed you?

For Jeremiah, it was prophetic proclamation, and God gave him the temperament he needed for that mission.

Which temperament are you—sanguine, choleric, melancholy, phlegmatic? Which blend of inborn traits fits you for the lifework to which you are ordained?

Whatever the answer, it is part of your beauty. . .if it is surrendered to God and controlled by His Spirit.

Day 228

THE ULTIMATE LOVE

This is how God showed his love among us:
He sent his one and only Son into the world
that we might live through him.

1 JOHN 4:9 NIV

∽

We don't have to try to grab hold of intangible proof of God's love. He sent it to us in the physical body of Jesus. Jesus was the love of God walking on earth. God blesses us in countless ways; He expresses His love through the many, many good things in our lives. But the ultimate expression of His love is still Jesus.

YOU ARE PART OF SOMETHING BIG

The suffering won't last forever. It won't be long before this generous God who has great plans for us in Christ—eternal and glorious plans they are!— will have you put together and on your feet for good. He gets the last word; yes, he does.

1 PETER 5:10–11 MSG

❧

No circumstance or person will ever be strong enough to push our God out of the way. Even His haters will ultimately bow their knees before His throne. So when the going gets tough, always remember that, in the end, God wins.

Day 230
HE CONTROLS THE END

I will cry unto God most high; unto God that performeth all things for me.

PSALM 57:2 KJV

❧

God "performs" all things for me. In Hebrew, it is the idea of bringing something to an end, to complete it. He perfects all things and sees that they accomplish His will. We are not robots, but we are sovereignly being directed toward an expected or anticipated end. We do not need to thrash around wondering what all the details of life add up to; He knows. We cry out and He performs His will. How comforting is that?

Day 231
CELEBRATING YOU

Her clothing is fine linen and purple.
PROVERBS 31:22 NKJV

Yeah, girlfriend, you have style. Your own. The way you put together your colors and patterns and textures and accessories. You have a unique way of wearing your beauty.

God gave that to you. He put inside you a brand that only you can express. Of course, that doesn't mean He is glorified by weirdness or sloppiness or dirtiness or seductiveness. But when we steward our beauty well, He looks good and so do we.

Today, celebrate your style by honoring Him.

A WELL OF JOY

When he arrived and saw this evidence of
God's blessing, he was filled with joy.
ACTS 11:23 NLT

❦

One of the spiritual blessings God gives us is joy—
and all His other blessings increase that joy. Joy is
like a spring of water that keeps spilling into our
lives. Just when we think the spring has run dry,
when we feel as though we'll never feel joy again,
joy wells up. At first, it may just be a tiny trickle—but
then it grows into a rushing stream that fills our
hearts once more.

YOU CAN ASK FOR UNDERSTANDING

[That] the eyes of your understanding being enlightened; that ye may know what is the hope of his calling, and what the riches of the glory of his inheritance in the saints.

EPHESIANS 1:18 KJV

Every day we are presented with new opportunities and unique decisions where we don't know what to do. In these situations, pray what Paul prayed: "God, please open my understanding to Your will." Trust that He will show you exactly what you need to know—and if the situation involves others, you can pray for them too!

Day 234
PRAYING FOR YOUR CHILDREN

The fear of the LORD is the beginning of wisdom,
and the knowledge of the Holy
One is understanding.
PROVERBS 9:10 NASB

We should be confident that the Lord loves hearing mothers praying scripture with their children in mind. This verse in Proverbs might be paraphrased, "Lord, cause my children to fear You, since this is the beginning of wisdom. Add years to their lives as they learn to have Your perspective on any situation." There are hundreds of passages like this that can be used to pray on behalf of our children. It's powerful. Let's try it today.

Day 235
BE A CROWN

A virtuous and worthy wife [earnest and strong in character] is a crowning joy to her husband, but she who makes him ashamed is as rottenness in his bones.

PROVERBS 12:4 AMPC

Wives can be crowns, and they can be cancers. They can bring shining honor to the men to whom they are married or eat away at the very core of manhood.

Even if you are unmarried today, you can be a woman of beautiful character, a woman who possesses the inner loveliness to crown another with glory.

God wants to use you to shine for Him. Start today.

Day 236
BLESSED WITH LAUGHTER

You make known to me the path of life;
you will fill me with joy in your presence,
with eternal pleasures at your right hand.

PSALM 16:11 NIV

Here, the Hebrew word is *samach*, which means joy in the sense of "mirth"—the sort of happiness that makes you laugh out loud. Our faith is not meant to be a gloomy, stern thing, filled with disapproval and a constant "No." Instead, those of us who follow Jesus say "Yes!" to life. We enjoy life! We smile and laugh a lot—because we know the pleasures God shows us will last throughout eternity.

Day 237
YOU CAN EMBRACE CHANGE

For you know that when your faith is tested,
your endurance has a chance to grow.
JAMES 1:3 NLT

I hate change. The problem is, we want a new house.
In order to make this journey easier, I need to view
it as a chance to grow.

My trust in God will increase as we search for
the right home. It'll be stretched again as we wait
for the buyer who wants to purchase our home.
Because this will strengthen my patience and trust
in God, I will ask God for help to embrace
change.

Day 238
LOVE OTHERS LIKE YOU LOVE YOURSELF

You do well when you complete the Royal Rule of the Scriptures: "Love others as you love yourself."
JAMES 2:8 MSG

～

We all know how to love and dote on ourselves. But if we want to fulfill God's grand plan for our lives, we need to follow the Royal Rule and consider the needs of others. We need to give generously (not just when we deem someone worthy). We need to forgive (even when we were clearly wronged). We need to avoid gossip and slander (speaking kindly even to the mean spirited). So who needs your love today?

HE REALLY SEES YOU

---

*God has said: "I will never
leave you nor forsake you."*

HEBREWS 13:5 PHILLIPS

❧

Rejection is hard.

If you've been rejected after tryouts for a sports team, musical auditions, creative writing submissions, college applications, or job interviews, you know the pain.

Personal rejections hurt even more: your mom didn't want you; your boyfriend found someone else; your husband took another woman to his heart; your child wants nothing to do with you. These rejections strike at the heart of our womanhood.

But God sees in you a beauty that the foolish rejections of others cannot diminish.

Day 240
SPRINGTIME JOY

Shout for joy to the LORD, all the earth,
burst into jubilant song.

PSALM 98:4 NIV

❧

This verse uses yet another Hebrew word: *patsach*,
which means "to makes something burst open, to
break forth." It makes me think of a spring day, when
green buds are opening on every twig, and every
bird and frog is singing at the top of its lungs. God
blesses us with springtime joy, the sort of joy that
can't be contained. It breaks open our hard hearts,
letting joy and life spill out of us into the world.

Day 241
YOU CAN ASK

"Keep on asking, and you will receive what you ask for. Keep on seeking, and you will find. Keep on knocking, and the door will be opened to you."

MATTHEW 7:7 NLT

With all the emphasis God places on prayer in the Bible, it's funny we sometimes forget to ask God for simple things. We don't need to relegate prayer to "big" things. We also don't need to stop asking because we don't see the answer we want. We can ask God for anything and keep bringing our prayers before Him. He'll answer our prayers!

Day 242
CHERISHING OUR FRIENDS

Do not forsake your own friend.
PROVERBS 27:10 NASB

When Aristotle said that friendship is a single soul in two bodies, he must have had women in mind. Growing old with a dear best friend is an incredible blessing. They stimulate us and encourage us. They are like a mirror; we see ourselves in a clearer way when we spend time with them. They remind us of God's faithfulness and provide support, all the while loving us unconditionally. Cherish that special friend. Give her a call right now and tell her, "I thank my God upon every remembrance of you. . . ."

Day 243
ENDLESS PROCESS

*Being confident of this very thing, that He who
has begun a good work in you will complete
it until the day of Jesus Christ.*

PHILIPPIANS 1:6 NKJV

The growing process includes awkward stages, whether in plants, animals, or humans. Fragile green sprouts hardly have the lush contours of ripe vegetables; spindly pupa and tiny tadpoles do not look like their adult destiny, and the oversized heads and pudgy legs of human toddlers are cute but not streamlined.

Womanhood, like other growth, is a process. God began it in you when you were conceived and continues it to this very day.

Day 244
DAWN

"The people living in darkness have seen a great
light; on those living in the land of the shadow
of death a light has dawned."

MATTHEW 4:16 NIV

∽

We often feel as though we're stumbling around
in the dark. We'd like to follow God, but we're
overwhelmed by sorrows and discouragement. We
don't know which way to turn. But if we're patient,
even the darkest nights give way to the dawn.
God's light will rise in our lives once again—and all
the shadows will disappear.

Day 245
YOU DON'T HAVE TO KNOW WHEN

So let's not get tired of doing what is good.
At just the right time we will reap a harvest
of blessing if we don't give up.
GALATIANS 6:9 NLT

⤳

I'm one of many moms who has a baby in heaven.
Brody Mark came at twenty-one weeks. My arms
ached the months following his birthday; I couldn't
fathom feeling right again. Now I have my arms full
with his two brothers. I didn't know when it would
happen, but my day came.

Keep trusting God with your heart. Your
day will come too.

Day 246
DEVOTED TO ONE ANOTHER

Be devoted to one another in brotherly love.
ROMANS 12:10 NASB

⌒

When an elephant is under duress, another elephant will stick its trunk in the sad one's mouth. It's a touch that seems to say, "I am here to help you." And still another elephant will start a chirping noise that seems to convey, "You don't have to go through this alone." Animal behavior is so instructive. Paul was equally instructive when he told the Romans to be devoted to one another. This devotion is a kind of affection that can be seen by others. Who needs to hear you chirp today?

Day 247
BEAUTIFUL LIKE ZION

Out of Zion, the perfection of beauty,
God hath shined.

PSALM 50:2 KJV

I have likened the daughter of Zion
to a comely and delicate woman.

JEREMIAH 6:2 KJV

Zion is the symbol of God's presence, His dwelling place. The "daughter of Zion" is a biblical name for Jerusalem, the Holy City.

God chose to characterize these hallowed places using the idea of beauty. Our God created and blesses the concept of holy beauty. You were created to reflect it.

Today, choose to let His holiness illuminate your life and make you beautiful.

Day 248
HEART SEARCHING

Search me, O God, and know my heart; try me and know my anxious thoughts; and see if there be any hurtful way in me, and lead me in the everlasting way.

PSALM 139:23–24 NASB

Asking for divine guidance isn't like consulting a Magic 8 Ball. We don't get immediate answers. Instead, we need time alone with God, time when we open our hearts to Him. We have to be honest—with Him and with ourselves—willing to see our unhealthy thoughts and wrong behavior. Only then will He be able to bless us with His guidance.

Day 249
YOU DON'T HAVE TO UNDERSTAND

Trust in the LORD with all thine heart;
and lean not unto thine own understanding.
PROVERBS 3:5 KJV

When Pastor Nate Ruch's son was a toddler, he gashed his forehead on a table. The ER was understaffed, so Pastor Nate had to hold David so the doctor could numb him before stitches. As David watched the needle come close, he was confused. *Dad, what are you doing to me?* He didn't understand; he had to trust his father.

We don't always understand God's actions, but we can be confident He knows what is best.

Day 250
MARRIAGE IS HONORABLE

Marriage is honourable in all,
and the bed undefiled.

HEBREWS 13:4 KJV

&

We live in a world of throwaway commitments. One city recently proposed temporary marriage licenses as an alternative to plunging into a lifetime of faithfulness. God's plan is one woman for one man, and it is an honorable plan. We can't survive in a culture where vows mean nothing. Today is a great day to thank God for your husband and pray for him (warts and all).

Day 251
SUPPORT WHEN NEEDED

*Cast your burden on the LORD,
and He shall sustain you.*

PSALM 55:22 NKJV

❧

Sometimes we women just need a little support!

Life has many details to manage and people to nurture. As the God-gifted multitaskers in the family, women are pretty good at juggling schedules and meals and errands and appointments. But we also have burdens. And it is hard to revel in the beauty of life if we're bogged down with stuff. So the Father tells us to let Him help us carry the load.

Today, He wants you to know that you are not alone.

Day 252
LET THERE BE LIGHT!

For God, who commanded the light to shine out of darkness, hath shined in our hearts, to give the light of the knowledge of the glory of God in the face of Jesus Christ.

2 CORINTHIANS 4:6 KJV

Humans have always loved light. Since the beginning of the twentieth century, starting with Einstein, physicists have been discovering amazing things about light that make it even more mysterious, even more wonderful. And God created it! If He could create light out of darkness and nothingness, He can shine the blessing of spiritual light into even the darkest hearts.

Day 253
YOU DON'T HAVE TO KNOW THE REASON

---

*"My thoughts are nothing like your thoughts,"
says the LORD. "And my ways are far
beyond anything you could imagine."*

ISAIAH 55:8 NLT

I vividly remember when I had the unusual thought to turn one street earlier than normal on my way to school. I dismissed the thought as silly. When I saw that the road I normally turn on was blocked by a police car, I rethought my actions.

God is always directing our steps in simple ways. Our job is to tune out our heads and tune in to our hearts.

Day 254
A MIND TO WORK

So we built the wall and the whole wall was joined together to half its height, for the people had a mind to work.

NEHEMIAH 4:6 NASB

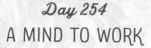

Negative people poison the workplace. Positive, encouraging workers, on the other hand, ignite one another's efforts. Creativity flows, energy multiples, and they produce results. So it was with the wall in Jerusalem. People had "a mind to work." Literally, they had the will to focus on the job at hand. They ignored the critical voices and got after it. Attitude mattered then, and it does now. Do you have a mind to work today?

Day 255
THE EYES HAVE IT

"How beautiful you are, my love,
how beautiful! Your eyes are soft as doves."
SONG OF SOLOMON 1:15 TLB

We all want beautiful eyes. And there is no shortage of tips on how to make the most of them. But, regardless of the color or size or depth of the ones you have, they are beautiful because God picked them for you.

Go look at your eyes. Everything about them says He designed you specifically for His glory. Let His light make them beautiful today.

Day 256
BODY AND SOUL

Beloved, I pray that in all respects you
may prosper and be in good health,
just as your soul prospers.

3 JOHN 1:2 NASB

❧

The New Testament makes clear that God sends both physical and spiritual blessings into our lives. He wants our lives to be healthy and prosperous—emotionally, physically, financially, spiritually. We tend to separate the spiritual world from the physical one, but the Bible shows us a perspective where each sort of blessing flows into all the others. As we are spiritually blessed, our physical lives will be blessed as well.

YOU CAN TUNE YOUR HEART TO GOD

"But the Helper, the Holy Spirit, whom the Father will send in my name, he will teach you all things and bring to your remembrance all that I have said to you."

JOHN 14:26 ESV

The Holy Spirit is constantly talking to you, prompting you to remember the Bible in different situations you face. He even helps you in your daily tasks. The urge to make sure you didn't leave your wallet on the kitchen counter? That's often Him! The more you recognize Him, the more you hear Him and learn to respond.

Day 258
CARING FOR GRANDCHILDREN

May you live to see your children's children.
PSALM 128:6 NIV

❧

Having grandchildren is one of life's greatest joys. And having them live with you is a special blessing. It can be a great deal of work, but what a privilege to be so involved with those little ones. Let's treasure our time with them. Let's make a significant investment in them as we talk and share our life experiences. It is a treat to be spiritual role models. So as we stick godly fingerprints all over their souls, let's faithfully pray for them.

QUIRKILY LOVELY

For He knows our frame,
He [earnestly] remembers and imprints
[on His heart] that we are dust.

PSALM 103:14 AMPC

Just a handful of dust. That's you. But beautiful dust, because the Creator chose and formed it and imbued it with His own breath.

Dust has its lowly attributes. And you have yours. Your family, friends, and coworkers know them well, those oddities of your personality that make them raise an eyebrow or stifle a chuckle.

Maybe He smiles too, but always with eyes of love. Those quirks identify our unique beauty.

Day 260
RELENTLESS LOVE

I am convinced that nothing can ever separate us from God's love. Neither death nor life, neither angels nor demons, neither our fears for today nor our worries about tomorrow—not even the powers of hell can separate us from God's love.

ROMANS 8:38 NLT

You can turn your eyes away from God. You can insist on shutting your heart against Him. But God's love is unstoppable and relentless. It leaks into the cracks of your heart. It waits patiently for you to turn around and notice it's there. It is always ready to bless you.

Day 261
YOU CAN TURN YOUR
THOUGHTS INTO PRAYER

Pray without ceasing.
1 THESSALONIANS 5:17 KJV

Whether it's natural disasters, a horrible crime, or a celebrity's recent struggles, the media is always telling us what's happening in this world—and a lot of times it isn't good. When I find myself dwelling too long on what is happening, I am learning to turn my thoughts into prayers. I can pray for people whom I will never meet, and I believe God will hear my prayers and impact their lives in some way.

Day 262
IT'S NOT ENOUGH TO JUST LOVE GOD

And he has given us this command:
Anyone who loves God must also
love their brother and sister.

1 JOHN 4:21 NIV

In most homes, sibling rivalry is alive and well. And this verse could help control the bickering, but that's not its primary purpose. Actually, John is trying to underscore the truth that it's not enough to just love the Lord. We have to also love those around us. This love (*agape*) is expressed when we find our joy in blessing someone else and not ourselves. When we love the Lord, we show it by the way we treat others.

BEAUTIFULLY OPEN

"A good man out of the good treasure of his heart brings forth good; and an evil man out of the evil treasure of his heart brings forth evil. For out of the abundance of the heart his mouth speaks."

LUKE 6:45 NKJV

God's grace at work gives us the strength to be vulnerable and open, to share the "treasure" within, our inner beauty, thoughts, dreams, and longings. Satan wants to wall up our beauty, to make us closed and fearful, bitter and cynical. But Christ conquered him and gives us the grace to be beautifully open, reflecting Him.

LEAP FOR JOY!

"Blessings await you when people hate you and exclude you and mock you and curse you as evil because you follow the Son of Man. When that happens, be happy! Yes, leap for joy!"

LUKE 6:22–23 NLT

This is quite a promise! The word Jesus uses is *skirtaó*, which means literally "leap for joy." It's also the word used when a baby "quickens," when the mother first feels the movement of life. So Jesus is saying this: if you follow Him and feel misunderstood and separated from everyone around you, that's the very moment new joy will leap into life!

Day 265
YOU DON'T HAVE TO AGREE

---

*And David danced before the L*ORD *with all his might. . . . So David and all the people of Israel brought up the Ark of the L*ORD *with shouts of joy.*
2 SAMUEL 6:14–15 NLT

King David had watched Uzzah die when he touched the Ark of the Covenant three months prior to the verses found in 2 Samuel. David had been angry and afraid of God, but he didn't allow either feeling to stay. The draw of the Lord's presence was strong, and David allowed his trust in the Lord to be limitless. That's what he focused on when he praised.

LIVING LIFE WITH OTHERS

And Ruth said, Intreat me not to leave thee,
or to return from following after thee:
for whither thou goest, I will go;
and where thou lodgest, I will lodge.

RUTH 1:16 KJV

This verse is often found on the inside of wedding bands, but in context, it's a daughter-in-law committing herself to "doing life" with her mother-in-law. Ruth is promising to be an integral part of Naomi's life. God never intended for His kids to live the solitary life. His plan is for us to be in a community, to know others and to be known.

Day 267
BEST BEAUTY SECRET

Yes, all of you be submissive to one another,
and be clothed with humility, for "God resists
the proud, but gives grace to the humble."

1 PETER 5:5 NKJV

"If you've got it, flaunt it."

That's the philosophy of the culture around us. We are encouraged to use our beauty for our own means, to draw attention to ourselves for our own indulgence.

God says for us to be clothed, not with our own pride, but with humility. This attitude comes from His grace within, the best beauty secret around.

Day 268
PEACE COVENANT

I give unto him my covenant of peace.
NUMBERS 25:12 KJV

❧

We humans make a lot of promises. We also break a lot of promises. Even when we start out with the best of intentions, we all too often find that we can't follow through with whatever we promised. God's promises are different from ours, though. When the Bible talks about a covenant, it's referring to a binding promise that can never be broken. God's promise of peace is a solid thing, firm and unchanging. It's a covenant that will never be broken.

Day 269
YOU DON'T HAVE TO KNOW HOW

But my God shall supply all your need according to his riches in glory by Christ Jesus.

PHILIPPIANS 4:19 KJV

Ryan and Brandi needed to move to a two-bedroom apartment; they prayed specifically for a monthly rent of $800.

The landlords at the apartments they liked discounted the regular $900 rent to $850. Although tempted to agree, Ryan and Brandi trusted God to answer their initial prayer. Within thirty minutes, the landlords called back; they liked them so much they agreed to the $800 rent.

Although you may not know how, God can answer your prayers.

Day 270
OUR OBEDIENCE AFFECTS OUR WORK

The Lord will send a blessing on your barns and on everything you put your hand to.
DEUTERONOMY 28:8 NIV

This passage begins in verses 1–2 with the statement that "If you fully obey the Lord.... All these blessings will come on you." There is a direct correlation between our character and God's blessing on our work. We can't expect to prosper when our hearts are not attuned to Him. That blessing we seek is a form of God's favor on the righteous. So, before you head off to work, check your heart, and then seek that blessing.

Day 271
FIXED ON THAT DAY

Surely goodness and mercy shall follow me
all the days of my life: and I will dwell
in the house of the Lᴏʀᴅ for ever.

PSALM 23:6 KJV

In God's presence, we will see how He worked in
us all along. We will delight in the knowledge that
He led us all the way, that it was His hand that
sculpted and fashioned us and His goodness and
mercy that followed us.

Don't despair, no matter what you see today.
Keep your eyes fixed on that day when you
will forever be in His house.

Day 272
GOD'S NATURE

Surely you have granted him unending blessings.
PSALM 21:6 NIV

❧

Unending. The Bible uses that word over and over, telling us again and again that eternity and blessing are part of God's very nature. His being has no end, no limits. And since God is love (1 John 4:8), His love is constantly flowing around us and into us—an unending stream of blessings.

Day 273
DIFFICULTY IS COMING

You did it: you changed wild lament into whirling dance; you ripped off my black mourning band and decked me with wildflowers.

PSALM 30:11 MSG

Life can be intimidating. A bad doctor's report or financial difficulty can turn your world upside down. But just as quickly as negative circumstances come into our lives, we can always remind ourselves that anything can happen. God can turn our lives around in moments.

Keep focused on Him; He will bring you through.

Day 274
ANNOUNCING GOOD NEWS

*How lovely on the mountains are the feet of him
who brings good news, who announces peace
and brings good news of happiness.*

ISAIAH 52:7 NASB

Once we have embraced the message of the Gospel, it's our turn to go and become publishers of peace. If we had the cure for cancer, we would not keep it to ourselves. Since the truth of the Gospel is so much more important, let's start sharing good news. Is there someone struggling at work? Does a friend need forgiveness? Is a neighbor alone with their fears? Let's go tell it on the mountain—real peace is available!

Day 275
RADIANT REFLECTION

But we all, with unveiled face, beholding as in a mirror the glory of the Lord, are being transformed into the same image from glory to glory, just as by the Spirit of the Lord.

2 CORINTHIANS 3:18 NKJV

Though our vision isn't what God can see, even our earthly eyes can recognize that we are being transformed a little more every day into a reflection of Him. Through His grace, through our trials and testings, through our faith, we are being conformed to His beautiful image.

Today, hold on to the radiant progress you see!

Day 276
GOD'S FAITHFUL LOVE

I cry out, "My splendor is gone! Everything I had hoped for from the LORD is lost!" The thought of my suffering. . .is bitter beyond words. I will never forget this awful time, as I grieve over my loss. Yet I still dare to hope when I remember this: The faithful love of the LORD never ends! His mercies never cease.

LAMENTATIONS 3:18–22 NLT

God's blessing isn't like an eternal raincoat that protects us from sorrow. Awful times will come. We will grieve over losses. And yet, even then, we can be confident that God's love is faithful. We live in eternity—and God is still blessing us.

OUR PERMANENT HOME IS COMING

So we don't look at the troubles we can see now;
rather, we fix our gaze on things that cannot be
seen. For the things we see now will soon be gone,
but the things we cannot see will last forever.

2 CORINTHIANS 4:18 NLT

My grandpa Carl lived for three years longer than his
wife of sixty-three years. During that time, I watched
him embody the truth that earth is temporary. He
knew he would soon meet with his wife in heaven
and bow together before our Lord.

May we live knowing heaven is near.

Day 278
PEACEFUL SLEEP

I will both lay me down in peace, and sleep:
for thou, Lᴏʀᴅ, only makest me dwell in safety.
PSALM 4:8 KJV

Insomnia is a huge problem for women. And the usual remedies of avoiding caffeine, following a set routine for bedtime, and keeping our rooms dark and cold may not solve the problem. When we are stirred with fears and frustrations, only the Lord can clear a path to restful, rejuvenating sleep. He does so by making us rest in "safety." He is awake and providing our security; we get peaceful sleep. Take Him up on it tonight!

Day 279
WRINKLES NO MORE

Who will transform our lowly body that it may be conformed to His glorious body, according to the working by which He is able even to subdue all things to Himself.

PHILIPPIANS 3:21 NKJV

❧

Wrinkles are a thing of earth. Yay! Add to that list all the warts and blemishes and bumps and lumps and diseases and disorders that make up the laundry list of human ailments, and you have what the apostle Paul called a "lowly body."

Today, rejoice in the knowledge that you will be beautiful for eternity—in a new body!

STAY CONNECTED

"*Your Father knows exactly what you need even before you ask him!*"

MATTHEW 6:8 NLT

❧

We need to pray. The Bible tells us to "pray without ceasing" (1 Thessalonians 5:17 KJV). But we don't pray because God needs to be told what we need. We pray because we need to be in vital connection with God; we need to be always aware that we are living in eternity. But God already knows what we need, better than we do ourselves. We don't need to give directions as to how He should bless us!

Day 281
THE NEED FOR WISDOM IS COMING

Some things Paul writes are difficult to understand.
Irresponsible people who don't know what they
are talking about twist them every which way.

2 PETER 3:16 MSG

We're living in a time when people come up with
both convincing and crazy reasons why the Bible
isn't real. We need wisdom from God to know
how to sense what is truth, what isn't, and how to
respond to both. If you're in that situation right
now, pray for God's wisdom. He will respond!

Day 282
SHALOM

I will listen to what God the LORD says;
he promises peace to his people.

PSALM 85:8 NIV

❧

In the Old Testament, the Hebrew word for "peace" is *shalom*. Peace can exist between people, nations, and God and His people. The foundation of that peace is a covenant or kind of promise. In this verse, God makes sure we understand that His peace is the result of Him keeping a promise. It is not the result of our work. Our job is to listen to what He says. Are you experiencing shalom right now? Are you listening to Him?

Day 283
YOU ARE A MICRO WITNESS

And he is before all things,
and by him all things consist.
COLOSSIANS 1:17 KJV

There is nothing in this life that is not touched by God. He is the source; He is the energy; He is the constancy.

At times, matters of faith are seen as outdated and irrelevant to the modern discussion. Concepts like evolution seem to sidestep His relevance. But you are a witness that He is very present in your life and that because there is micro-involvement of the divine, there must also be macro-involvement of the same.

RICHNESS OF LIFE

The blessing of the LORD makes a person rich.
PROVERBS 10:22 NLT

⌒

The Hebrew word used here for "makes rich" is *ashar*, which means "creates abundance." When we talk about blessing, that's what we really mean— the abundant riches, thriving health, overflowing bounty that God pours into our lives in countless shapes and forms, myriad varieties, all the depth and width that's contained in eternity. This richness of life is what God's blessings create for us and in us. This is the life we enter into through Jesus.

TRIBULATION IS COMING

---

*"So when all these things begin to happen,
stand and look up, for your salvation is near!"*

LUKE 21:28 NLT

Terrorism, bullies, criminals, natural disasters—this world is filled with negative circumstances that can overwhelm our lives with fear and worry. When that happens to me, I walk outside and look up. I stare at the sky, clouds, and sun. The Creator of those natural things created my heart and my life. He knows exactly what is going on in this world—and He knows how to keep you and me safe.

---

*Now may the Lord of peace himself give you
peace at all times and in every way.*

2 THESSALONIANS 3:16 NIV

It is human nature to try to find loopholes in agreements. When we read this verse, we might be tempted to try to think of an exception when the Lord might not provide His peace in a given situation. But just to make sure we walk through life and pursue His purposes with complete assurance, Paul uses terms like "at all times" and "in every way." Peace for every situation we may face. Wow.

Day 287
THE WITNESS OF KINDNESS

She opens her mouth with wisdom,
and on her tongue is the law of kindness.
PROVERBS 31:26 NKJV

❧

There is no beauty without kindness.

A razor-sharp tongue quickly destroys any attractiveness that would otherwise be seen. Cutting words and careless comments are the way to prove that there is no inner beauty of soul.

Jesus called us to love, to speak gentle words, to practice forgiveness and mercy. Women who make sure to guard their words are women who truly understand beauty.

Day 288
PRAISE SONG

---

*Let all that I am praise the L*ORD*; may I never forget the good things he does for me. He forgives all my sins and heals all my diseases. He redeems me from death and crowns me with love and tender mercies. He fills my life with good things.*

PSALM 103:2–5 NLT

Since all these eternal blessing are ours, our entire being should sing with praise!

Day 289
STRENGTH THROUGH MEEKNESS

We find ourselves. . .not needing to
force our way in life.
GALATIANS 5:22–23 MSG

As the Spirit continues to increase your faithfulness, you start to realize that forcefulness is not a virtue. Meekness is. Some people associate meekness with weakness or backing down, but the opposite is actually true. Meekness provides the strength you need to stand in the position God has placed you. Humility allows you to confidently pursue God's purpose, knowing God will open the opportunities you need to make that happen. Without Him, you can do nothing; with Him, you can do all things.

Day 290
THERE WILL BE DIFFICULTIES

"In this godless world you will continue to experience difficulties. But take heart! I've conquered the world."

JOHN 16:33 MSG

Most of us want to believe that pursuing God's purpose for our lives automatically earns us a "get out of jail free" card. No more problems for us! But that isn't how it works. Instead, Christ promises to "conquer" those difficulties. Literally, He promises to subdue or overcome them and render us victorious in spite of the anguish. He stands with us in the midst of the junk. Good deal!

YOU TELL OF HIS PLAN

It is he who saved us and chose us for his holy work not because we deserved it but because that was his plan long before the world began—to show his love and kindness to us through Christ.

2 TIMOTHY 1:9 TLB

God planned for you to be His long ago. Before even a cell of your body was present on this earth, you were very present in His plan.

Through His Son, God reached out to us with love and kindness. In this He offered us what no one else could. And today, He is still working to bring that plan to beautiful completion.

Day 292
KEYS TO THE KINGDOM

---

*"It gives your Father great happiness
to give you the Kingdom."*

LUKE 12:32 NLT

༒

Sometimes when we pray, we act as though God is
a stingy, distant authority figure. We plead with Him
to give us the things we need. We beg Him to bless
us. But we don't need to pray like that. Instead, we
can pray with confidence. We don't have to beg.
It makes God happy to bless us. God's Kingdom
is rich and full, immense and lovely—and He wants
to give us the whole entire thing!

Day 293
PATIENCE IS A VIRTUE

But what happens when we live God's way? . . .
We develop a willingness to stick with things.
GALATIANS 5:22–23 MSG

When I'm at church or out with my boys, I'm often tempted to check my phone. Every time I do, though, I'm letting impatience rule me. I'm not focusing on and enjoying the moment I'm in.

When we let God's Spirit reside in us, we continue to strengthen our patience muscle. We learn to stick with listening, forgiveness, and grace. We can focus on the moment because we know God is at work.

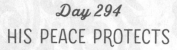

Day 294
HIS PEACE PROTECTS

And the peace of God, which passeth all
understanding, shall keep your hearts
and minds through Christ Jesus.
PHILIPPIANS 4:7 KJV

Paul uses a strong word to describe how God's peace can protect our emotions. Our minds are not just "being kept"; they are guarded. Think about two huge soldiers standing post outside each of our hearts. When worry and anxiety begin to monopolize our emotions, we need help. We need to call on the guards. And the peace of God will invade our souls, putting our hearts at rest.

Day 295
REDEEMED STATEMENT

I will ransom them from the power of the grave;
I will redeem them from death.

HOSEA 13:14 KJV

୨୧

If you belong to Christ, you have been redeemed from the very jaws of eternal death. And that is a powerful witness. Our world lives in fear—and with good reason. It is a very unsafe, unstable world. But we—who know the Lord of life and whom the grave no longer holds captive—are God's showcase.

Today, your trust in Him as you approach life with all its uncertainties is a beautiful statement of His redemption.

Day 296
UNFOLDING GOD'S TABLECLOTH

Not a day goes by without his unfolding grace.
2 CORINTHIANS 4:16 MSG

Imagine a tablecloth folded tightly into a small square, only a few inches across. As you start to unfold it, however, you realize it's not small at all; it's actually long and wide. The more you unfold it, the longer and wider it becomes. God's blessings are like that: not a day goes by that He's not unfolding new expressions of His grace in your life. His tablecloth of blessing is longer and wider than anything you can imagine!

Day 297
RECOGNIZE THEIR BATTLE IS VALID

---

*Don't jump all over [fellow believers] every time
they do or say something you don't agree with. . . .
Remember, they have their own history to
deal with. Treat them gently.*

ROMANS 14:1 MSG

༄

When someone is battling something I've already
conquered, I need to remember what Paul writes
later in Romans 14 (MSG): "If there are corrections
to be made or manners to be learned, God can
handle that without your help."

Although our battles look different, we are
fighting the same war against the enemy—
and we all have been given the same
victory in Jesus!

Day 298
GREAT EAGERNESS

For they received the word with great eagerness,
examining the Scriptures daily.

ACTS 17:11 NASB

❧

What kinds of things do you look forward to with
great eagerness? Making a great meal for your
family? Planning a well-deserved vacation? Well,
in this verse, Paul is commending the church at
Berea for their eagerness to dive into the scriptures
every single day. *Eagerness* in Greek means to be
ready, to have "clarity of mind." He is commending
them for the daily discipline it takes to be in God's
Word. We can't follow His plan if we don't study
His Word with eagerness!

ESCAPE FROM THE TOWER

[The Father] has delivered and drawn us to Himself out of the control and the dominion of darkness and has transferred us into the kingdom of the Son of His love.

COLOSSIANS 1:13 AMPC

Don't ever forget that you had no chance of real love if Jesus had not come to die for you.

Like the fairy-tale princess in the tower, you had no hope of escape.

Jesus came and rescued you from the dominion of darkness. And now, if you have received Him, you are living in the kingdom of love with Him.

Day 300
FRUIT TREES

Blessed is the one. . .whose delight is in the law of the LORD. . . . That person is like a tree planted by streams of water, which yields its fruit in season and whose leaf does not wither.

PSALM 1:1–3 NIV

‿

When God gives us the blessing of His life, we thrive. We put down strong roots. God's life flows into us, the way trees pull water up from the earth into their branches and leaves. Even though we experience all the effects of this world's time, eternity keeps us green. Our lives are rich and fruitful.

Day 301

ARM YOURSELF WITH HOPE

And now there remain: faith. . .hope [confident
expectation of eternal salvation].
1 CORINTHIANS 13:13 AMP

∽

The idea of heaven has always provided hope for my future, but it has been magnified since my brother passed away. The hope of heaven keeps my feet moving and my heart at peace.

Whether you have loved ones there or are simply waiting for the day Jesus will take us home, let that hope of heaven fuel your future.

Day 302
GOD'S WORD ACCOMPLISHES
ITS PURPOSE

"So will the words that come out of my mouth not come back empty-handed. They'll do the work I sent them to do, they'll complete the assignment I gave them."

ISAIAH 55:11 MSG

&

As we seek to accomplish God's plan for our lives, we can follow the scriptures with confidence. In this verse, He is stating that His words do not return empty-handed or void. When needed, His Word directs or encourages or convicts or calms. It highlights mercy and promises justice. We can take it to the bank. His Word accomplishes His purposes. Let's turn it loose in our lives.

Day 303
BEAUTIFUL AND SPECIAL

For no one ever hated his own flesh,
but nourishes and cherishes it, just as
the Lord does the church.

EPHESIANS 5:29 NKJV

A man who loves his wife will take delight in making her more beautiful by giving her pretty clothing, buying her perfume and flowers, maybe giving her a day at the spa. This is a small reflection of the heart of God.

Jesus, our Bridegroom, nourishes us with His love and cherishes us in many ways. We are more beautiful when we look for the ways He is showing us that we are special to Him.

Day 304
THE SHADOW OF DEATH

"The people living in darkness have seen a great light; on those living in the land of the shadow of death a light has dawned."

MATTHEW 4:16 NIV

༄

Death is the great mystery, the dark unknown that shadows all life. For us, death means sorrow. It means losing the people we love. For us, it may mean fear, even terror. And there's no escaping it. Everyone we love will die, and our dying day will come to each one of us. But Jesus let us know that death is not the end. Night may fall—but a new dawn will come.

Day 305
RECOGNIZE REPRIMANDS

---

*And a wise friend's timely reprimand is like
a gold ring slipped on your finger.*
PROVERBS 25:12 MSG

No one likes to be reprimanded—but sometimes that is exactly what we need. It takes guts to speak up and suggest a change or gently berate someone, but if we never spoke up in this way, we would never have the opportunity to improve our lives.

By the way, if you are the one giving a reprimand, always remember what Paul said in Ephesians 4:15—speak the truth in love.

Day 306
STUFFING OUR FACES

Your words were found and I ate them,
and Your words became for me a joy.
JEREMIAH 15:16 NASB

෩

There is a petite mother in Texas who holds a world record for consuming two 72-ounce steaks along with a baked potato, a roll, some shrimp cocktail, and a salad all in less than fifteen minutes! Women love to eat. But instead of stuffing our faces with favorite foods, let's mirror the sentiment of the prophet Jeremiah. He "ate" the words of the Lord, and they filled his heart with joy. That kind of a meal can really satisfy our hearts. Bon appétit!

Day 307
HE WANTED YOU FIRST

We love him, because he first loved us.
1 JOHN 4:19 KJV

❧

Women like to be wooed and won. And men were designed to do the pursuing.

More than a beautiful gender distinction, this age-old drama actually reflects God's relationship with us. He saw us and wanted us. He made the first move—in creation—and then again in salvation. His eyes are always watching for us. He never tires of showing His love for us. The only way we can escape this incredible love is to run from Him. It is thrilling to be wanted by God.

Day 308
LEAVING IT ALL

"And everyone who has left houses or brothers or sisters or father or mother or children or farms for My name's sake, will receive many times as much, and will inherit eternal life."

MATTHEW 19:29 NASB

～

God calls us to live in loving relationship with others—and yet when Jesus talks like this, He sounds as though He's saying the exact opposite, as though He wants us to abandon our children and our parents, our homes and our work. What He's really talking about, though, is the absolute surrender of giving everything we love to Him. We're no longer in control. He is.

Day 309
A TUG TOWARD GOODNESS

We develop. . . a conviction that a basic
holiness permeates things and people.
GALATIANS 5:22–23 MSG

❧

After the Spirit stirs in us a sense of compassion,
that gentleness begins to see goodness in other
people. We start to focus on people's strengths,
not their weaknesses.

Your natural tendency may be to focus on
negative things, so don't be alarmed when you
sense this tug toward goodness as the Spirit grows
in you. Instead, let your thoughts turn in that
direction. It's God's goodness coming to
you so it can flow through you to others.

Day 310
VALUABLE BENEFITS

*For the L*ORD *gives wisdom.*
PROVERBS 2:6 NIV

~

Every now and again, American Express sends out nice glossy postcards to announce valuable new benefits. With each announcement, they want cardholders to feel better. They want us shoppers to know that now we have more access or more purchasing power or more travel options, or more everything. Well, if they can do that with a credit card, imagine what it would be like if we regularly received creative, well-written, enticing announcements about something really important. Oh yeah, we do! Let's open our Bibles and check out the valuable benefits!

Day 311
PREPARED PLACE

In my Father's house are many mansions: if it were not so, I would have told you. I go to prepare a place for you. And if I go and prepare a place for you, I will come again, and receive you unto myself; that where I am, there ye may be also.

JOHN 14:2–3 KJV

It isn't enough for the groom to love the bride; no, he wants to spend his life in relationship with her, to live with her in his house.

Jesus wants us to be with Him. He is getting things ready for the big day.

Day 312
THE WATER OF LIFE

The water that I shall give him shall be in him a well of water springing up into everlasting life.
JOHN 4:14 KJV

❧

In the New Testament, the Greek word used for "life" is *zoé*. HELPS Word-Studies gives this definition for how Jesus is using the word: "physical and spiritual life, all life throughout the universe, which always and only comes from and is sustained by God's self-existent life. The Lord intimately shares His gift of life with people, creating each in His image which gives all the capacity to know His eternal life."

RECOGNIZE WHEN RIGHT
DOESN'T MATTER

It's God we are answerable to. . .not each other.
That's why Jesus lived and died and then lived
again: so that he could be our Master across
the entire range of life and death, and free us
from the petty tyrannies of each other.

ROMANS 14:8–9 MSG

Being right boosts our pride, but it never encourages
the person who is wrong. Sometimes our best
interests are served when we realize the question
"Who's right?" doesn't need to be answered.
We're on the same team.

SPIRITUAL FLASHLIGHTS

Your word is a lamp for my feet,
a light on my path.
PSALM 119:105 NIV

There are penlights, rechargeable flashlights, lanterns, headlights, and colorful nightsticks. All of them are designed to light up the area where you are walking and help you avoid an accident. God's Word is just such a light for our lives. The everyday paths that we trudge down need illumination. We need to know which direction to choose and which danger to avoid. Grab your Bible and shed some light on your day.

THE WARRIOR OF YOUR HEART

---

*And he personally bore our sins in his own body
on the cross, so that we might be dead to sin
and be alive to all that is good.*

1 PETER 2:24 PHILLIPS

～

Christ died for us, giving up His life for ours.

In all the great romance tales, the warrior is willing to die for the sake of the beautiful maiden he wants to rescue. Jesus is that Warrior. He is not willing to let the Enemy have us. He was willing to fight to the death for us. What a love He has for you!

Day 316
HEALED

Store my commands in your heart.
If you do this, you will live many years,
and your life will be satisfying.

PROVERBS 3:1–2 NLT

Think about scripture. Dwell on it. Commit it to memory. Fill your mind with it. It will do you good. It will give you life! The Hebrew word that's been translated as *life* and *live* implies being restored to life after a serious illness. It's the sort of life that is so full, so healthy, that it really can't be measured in years. Hear God's words and you, too, will experience this life.

ARM YOURSELF WITH FAITH

But for right now, until that completeness,
we have three things to do to lead us toward
that consummation: Trust steadily in God,
hope unswervingly, love extravagantly.

1 CORINTHIANS 13:13 MSG

Faith is so foundational to our Christianity that Paul listed it both as a piece of God's armor and at the end of 1 Corinthians 13 as one of the three things we hold on to as we wait for heaven.

Never lose sight of the truth that your faith will change your life.

Day 318
A GOOD OLD AGE

*"You shall go to your fathers in peace;
you will be buried at a good old age."*
GENESIS 15:15 NASB

Based on the way we keep looking for the fountain of youth, most of us want to ignore the whole topic of death. Not Abraham, for he was going to die in peace and be buried at "a good old age." In Hebrew, this term implies a time that is appealing or pleasant to the senses, a time that is proper or even convenient. It's the right time. Because of Christ, we, too, will be buried at "a good old age." Nothing to fear!

Day 319
NOT MY WAY

"Where have you come from?" the Lord asked
Satan. *"From earth, where I've been watching
everything that's going on,"* Satan replied.

JOB 2:2 TLB

❧

Do you think God has asked Satan about you like
He did about Job?

Your surrendered beauty is a statement to the
devil as well as to human beings. When you obey
God's commands and allow Him to shine through
you, you are correcting what Eve did wrong. You are
being a human woman who chooses to be
beautiful God's way and not her own way.

Day 320
ABUNDANT LIFE

I am come that they might have life,
and that they might have it more abundantly.
JOHN 10:10 KJV

We've talked about many kinds of blessings. In the end, all those blessings, both spiritual and material, can be contained in the blessing Jesus is talking about here—abundant life. Eternal life doesn't merely go on forever. It's a life that has no limits, not in time, not in strength, not in love. It's a life that's deep and rich, full of countless blessings.

Day 321
FREE TO BE CONFIDENT

---

*I pray that your hearts will be flooded with light
so that you can understand the confident hope he
has given to those he called—his holy people
who are his rich and glorious inheritance.*

EPHESIANS 1:18 NLT

❧

God is love. He is forever with us. He is gracious and just. He wrote down all His promises in a book so we could have direction for our lives on this earth. He is unchangeable and all-powerful. In other words, you can be confident in His Word and in Him.

Day 322
DEALING WITH SIN IN OUR YOUTH

Flee also youthful lusts.
2 TIMOTHY 2:22 KJV

In each season of life, there are particular sins that "easily beset us" (Hebrews 12:1 KJV). But teenagers seem to have a particular boatload of challenges and temptations. Here Paul gave Timothy insight into how to deal with youthful lust. He told him to "flee" or, more specifically, run! At any age, the secret to dealing with a tough temptation is to run away quickly. No pausing, no conversations, no sharing, no dabbling—just run! Got your running shoes on today?

Day 323
THEY'RE EVERYWHERE!

For I am not ashamed of the gospel of Christ:
for it is the power of God unto salvation
to every one that believeth.

ROMANS 1:16 KJV

You know them. You see them at work, the gym, the grocery store, even in church. Scoffers may all begin their journeys because of a deep personal disappointment. Their feelings of resentment are not dealt with, and they develop a harsh view of anyone who would believe there is a God who cares.

Your beauty as a woman who shows the love of Christ in practical ways is a magnet to the truth.

Day 324
BLESSINGS NOW

The LORD shall increase you more and more, you and your children.

PSALM 115:14 KJV

❧

Eternal life waits for us on the other side of death— but it also expands our lives right now. It makes them fuller, wider, deeper. It gives us *more* life than we ever knew was possible. And this promise of eternal blessing isn't only ours. It's so big that it spreads out from us. It reaches our children too. The Lord's blessings have no limits.

ALL BY HIS SPIRIT

But what happens when we live God's way?
He brings gifts into our lives, much the same
way that fruit appears in an orchard.
GALATIANS 5:22 MSG

❧

Have you ever seen an apple tree straining to grow apples? Trees don't have to work hard to create fruit. As long as they stay connected to their roots, fruit will appear.

In the same way, when we stay connected to the Holy Spirit, we abide in the vine of our heavenly Father and we will bear the fruit of the Spirit we read about in Galatians chapter 5!

Day 326
FILLED UP

May the God of hope fill you with all joy
and peace as you trust in him.
ROMANS 15:13 NIV

After Thanksgiving dinner, everyone's stomach is filled up to the brim with delicious food. We might say, "We are stuffed." In a similar way, when we as believers put our regular, everyday trust in the Savior, we are stuffed or "filled up" with joy and peace. Pursuing the will of God and working at His plan for our lives is a full-time pursuit. But it has amazing results!

BETTER THAN THE SPA

Blessed are those who keep His testimonies,
who seek Him with the whole heart!

PSALM 119:2 NKJV

❧

Today, God wants you to see Him with your whole heart. He wants you to know that being in relationship with Him is the one way to fully realize your personal beauty. You may seek after many things, but only an ongoing pursuit of Him, His person, and His leading in your life will truly make you a more complete person.

Talking to Him every day is the way to seek Him. Prayer is better than the spa.

Day 328
OPENED FLOODGATES

"Test me in this," says the LORD Almighty,
"and see if I will not throw open the floodgates
of heaven and pour out so much blessing that
there will not be room enough to store it."

MALACHI 3:10 NIV

❧

The "law of attraction" says to think about what you
want; focus your thoughts on it, and the Universe
will give it to you. God tells us something different.
He says surrender all your demands. Let go of all
your ideas about what you think you need. When
you do, He will pour more blessings into your life
than you can even grasp.

ABLE TO REFLECT GOD'S LOVE

---

*Let us love one another, for love comes from
God. Everyone who loves has been born of
God and knows God. Whoever does not love
does not know God, because God is love.*

1 JOHN 4:7–8 NIV

I once prayed for my husband to encounter God's
love. Then I had a revelation: I am the way Erik
sees God's love.

Although it's easy to feel inadequate to properly
showcase God's love, that's exactly what we are
called to do for others. We lean on Him, and
He enables us to reflect His love.

Day 330
HE WON'T FORGET

For God is not unrighteous to forget
your work and labour of love.

HEBREWS 6:10 KJV

Often God's purpose for our lives is displayed in the way we serve others. In this verse, Paul uses two different Greek words (in English, *work* and *labor*) to convey the importance of our service. Interestingly, the term *work* comes from a root meaning "to wail or beat our breasts" in emotion. This is a service or labor that really matters to us. We are not serving out of some kind of obligation. We want to reach out and help. And God will not forget that effort.

Day 331
SUFFERING TO BE BEAUTIFUL

Now obviously no "chastening" seems pleasant at the time: it is in fact most unpleasant. Yet when it is all over we can see that [it] has quietly produced the fruit of real goodness in the characters of those who have accepted it in the right spirit.

HEBREWS 12:11 PHILLIPS

"You have to suffer to be beautiful."

My mom used to say these words to me when I, as a child, was protesting her efforts to fix my hair. The beauty routine God creates for us also involves some pain. But it has great reward. Let it work for you.

Day 332
GOD'S PLEASURE

Let them shout for joy, and be glad. . .let them say continually, Let the LORD be magnified, which hath pleasure in the prosperity of his servant.

PSALM 35:27 KJV

God's not stingy. He doesn't like to see us suffer. It makes Him happy to bless us with prosperity. When we truly believe we have a God who loves us like that, we can stop worrying so much about our bank accounts. Instead of stressing out every time we sit down to pay our bills, we can praise God, knowing it gives Him pleasure to supply what we need.

IMMERSE YOURSELF IN STORIES OF FAITH

Take the old prophets as your mentors. They put up with anything, went through everything, and never once quit, all the time honoring God.

JAMES 5:10–11 MSG

I always thought the Old Testament phrase "the God of Abraham, Isaac, and Jacob" was another name for God. It actually is an endurance principle in action. That phrase prompts people to remember what God has done for their faith heroes. If God can do it for Abraham, Isaac, and Jacob—and your parents, grandparents, or other faith heroes—He can do it for you!

Day 334
HOLIDAYS

A feast is made for laughter.
ECCLESIASTES 10:19 NKJV

ॐ

If you like holidays, you're not alone. Most of us enjoy something about them, whether it's just the break from work or the actual family time and food or the significance of the day itself. Holidays just seem a bit more joyful than the average day. But as far as you're concerned, God puts no more emphasis on a holiday than on a Monday. He celebrates the wonder of you every day.

ORPHANS AND WIDOWS

Religion that God our Father accepts as pure and faultless is this: to look after orphans and widows in their distress.

JAMES 1:27 NIV

⌒

James understood that religion is much more than a spiritual organization; it is an activity. It is an activity addressing the weakest among us. He used a Greek word to signify that these folks are being crushed and squeezed by the circumstances of their lives. Children without parents, single elderly women, and others compressed by their lot in life need relief. How can we provide some help today?

Day 336
FOR WOMEN ONLY

And behold, a woman who had suffered from a flow of blood for twelve years came up behind Him and touched the fringe of His garment; for she kept saying to herself, If I only touch His garment, I shall be restored to health. Jesus turned around and, seeing her, He said, Take courage, daughter! Your faith has made you well. And at once the woman was restored to health.

MATTHEW 9:20–22 AMPC

In that culture and because of the social mores related to purification under the Mosaic law, a woman with a menstrual disorder was socially unacceptable. Anyone who touched her was unclean. Yet this woman risked reaching out to Jesus. And He healed her.

Day 337
GOD'S MASTERPIECES

*The LORD God made all sorts of trees grow up
from the ground—trees that were beautiful
and that produced delicious fruit.*

GENESIS 2:9 NLT

At the beginning of the Bible in the book of Genesis, we learn that God created the natural world. Nature is His masterpiece, an endlessly beautiful expression of divine creativity. Each tree—pines and oaks, palms and willows, maples and tamarinds—all of them are God's love poems. They speak to us of His unending power and love.

Day 338
HE IS OUR FRIEND

And so it happened just as the Scriptures say:
"Abraham believed God, and God counted
him as righteous because of his faith."
He was even called the friend of God.

JAMES 2:23 NLT

❧

You can tell God secrets and complain about life.
You can praise Him and ask Him to change things.
Isn't it amazing that we can confidently approach
God, update Him on life, turn to Him in need, and
trust Him through thick and thin? He can be—and
wants to be!—your best friend.

Day 339
HIS COUNSEL STANDS

Declaring the end from the beginning, and from
ancient times the things that are not yet done,
saying, My counsel shall stand,
and I will do all my pleasure.

ISAIAH 46:10 KJV

⌒

God said it, case closed. His counsel (His words,
His law, His promises) has been given and can now
be leaned upon. In Hebrew, when a person's words
"stand," it means that they can be ratified. The case
is closed. Discussion over. As part of His plan for
us, God has secured our eternal home. We
can have a quiet confidence in that fact.

Day 340
LONGING FOR HEALTH

Have mercy upon me, O Lord;
for I am weak: O Lord, heal me.
PSALM 6:2 KJV

❧

Our culture reveres health and fitness. Trends of eating organic, taking whole food supplements, and using essential oils and herbs bear testament to our fascination with natural health.

But our society is also plagued with diseases of the body and mind. Your beauty does not rely on you being 100 percent healthy. Your beauty is not only of the body but mostly of the soul. No pain you feel can make it disappear.

HEAVEN AND EARTH ARE THE LORD'S

*Behold, the heaven and the heaven of heavens
is the LORD's thy God, the earth also,
with all that therein is.*

DEUTERONOMY 10:14 KJV

Sometimes we forget that the earth is the Lord's. He
has entrusted it to our care, but it is still His. When
we exploit it, when we pollute the sky, when we pour
poison into its waters, we are damaging something
that belongs to God, not us. We are failing to honor
and respect the great blessings He has given
us through the natural world.

Day 342
FIGHT FAIR

My dear children, let's not just talk
about love; let's practice real love.
1 JOHN 3:18 MSG

When you disagree with someone, always remember
to fight fair. Make sure you each understand the
"playing field": you love each other, want what is
best for that relationship, and consider each other
equals. You simply disagree.

When you fight fair, you value the other person
through your words, your tone, your attitude, and
even your actions while you disagree. So fight well,
and fight fair.

Day 343
A BETTER COUNTRY

*For those who say such things make it clear
that they are seeking a country of their own.*

HEBREWS 11:14 NASB

In this chapter, the writer of Hebrews extols the virtues of the heroes of the faith. He mentions the patriarchs by name and then acknowledges those name-less saints who died as pilgrims on earth. And he sums up his thoughts by declaring that they all are waiting for a country of their own, a more preferred place to call home. That is what heaven is for the child of God—home. Rooted in His plan for us is a heavenly place of rest. Are you ready to go?

Day 344
VICTORIOUS WARRIOR PRINCESS

Blessed be the LORD my Rock, who trains my hands for war, and my fingers for battle.
PSALM 144:1 NKJV

❧

You are beautiful in battle—a battle against the Enemy, Satan.

No doubt the warrior-king David was speaking here about actual physical battle; he waged a lot of them. But we can be just as sure that our heavenly King will prepare us to fight the wiles of the devil. No fiery dart has to take us down. He has trained us well.

You are more beautiful, more victorious than Joan of Arc. You are God's warrior-princess. Today, you stand.

Day 345
WORDLESS SERMONS

"Look at the birds of the air, that they do not sow, nor reap nor gather into barns, and yet your heavenly Father feeds them. Are you not worth much more than they? . . . Observe how the lilies of the field grow; they do not toil nor do they spin, yet I say to you that not even Solomon in all his glory clothed himself like one of these."

MATTHEW 6:26, 28–29 NASB

If you're worried about your finances, spend some time watching a robin—or looking at a flower. Both of them have something to tell you.

Day 346
IMMERSE YOURSELF IN THANKFULNESS

Thank God no matter what happens.
This is the way God wants you who
belong to Christ Jesus to live.
1 THESSALONIANS 5:18 MSG

❧

We're teaching our three-year-old he doesn't need to whine to get what he wants. Although he cried to get something as a baby, he's growing up. Whining is no longer appropriate.

As adults, our whining sounds more like complaining—and yes, it sounds like fingernails on a chalkboard whether you are three or forty-three. Instead of complaining, try thankfulness. It keeps God and all His good things in front of you.

Day 347
WHAT ARE WE FOCUSED ON?

Set your affection on things above,
not on things on the earth.
COLOSSIANS 3:2 KJV

To "set your affection" on something implies a real search or quest. Paul used a Greek term here that denotes a serious, active, and single-minded pursuit of something important. He is urging us to fix our spiritual eyes on heaven and not on the everyday details of this life. We are admonished to be heavenly minded. We are to strain, as it were, toward something much more valuable. What are you focused on today?

Day 348
KEEPING SILENT

Set a watch, O LORD, before my mouth;
keep the door of my lips.
PSALM 141:3 KJV

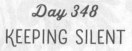

You are beautiful when you are silent. And you are beautiful when you speak. Knowing when to speak and when not to speak is so important.

Ecclesiastes 3 says there is a time for silence. If it is your time to do that, then being silent beautifies you the most right now. The Holy Spirit who lives within nudges us when we should not speak. Never ignore it.

Restraint of any kind is a sacrifice of action. But it usually makes you more beautiful.

Day 349
THE WORDS OF THE WISE

The words of the wise bring healing.
PROVERBS 12:18 NLT

None of us knows everything. No matter how mature we are in Christ, we all have times when our own knowledge runs out. We find ourselves confused, overwhelmed, weak. Times like those, we need friends and teachers, counselors and pastors who can share their wisdom with us. We need to be humble enough to ask for help—and then we need to be willing to open our minds and hearts to the healing we need.

Day 350
HE IS ABOVE ALL

God sits above the circle of the earth.
The people below seem like grasshoppers to him!
He spreads out the heavens like a curtain
and makes his tent from them.

ISAIAH 40:22 NLT

Some days I see life from God's perspective. My problems are microscopic and His power is prevalent. Other days I'm overwhelmed by what I'm facing just as an ant may feel walking through a cornfield.

When you're stuck seeing life through your perspective, imagine the Lord on His heavenly throne. Picture the realities of His power. That perspective will change your life.

Day 351
NOT HOME YET

Instead, they were longing for a
better country—a heavenly one.
HEBREWS 11:16 NIV

C. S. Lewis remarked, "If I find in myself a desire which no experience in this world can satisfy, the most probable explanation is that I was made for another world." Or as the old hymn says, "This world is not my home, I'm just a-passing through." As wives and mothers, it often falls to us to make a house a home. But if we sink our roots too deep into this world, we won't long for the next. Go ahead, review Revelation 22 and remind yourself what it's going to be like!

Day 352
DREAM HIS DREAMS

I realise that everyone has his own particular gift from God, some one thing and some another.

1 CORINTHIANS 7:7 PHILLIPS

❧

Most of us don't agree with the apostle that celibacy is a good thing. We long for romance, a meaningful relationship on which to build a marriage and family. But Paul said that some are gifted with singleness.

Christians are called to surrender, to acknowledge God's lordship over every area of our lives, even and especially this one.

Surrender your dreams of romance to the One who loves you most, and trust Him to give you a beautiful life in return.

Day 353
PAINFUL BLESSINGS

As iron sharpens iron,
so a friend sharpens a friend.
PROVERBS 27:17 NLT

Our friends can bring out the best in us. Sometimes that's a pleasant experience. We bask in the knowledge that someone truly understands and appreciates us. But a real friend doesn't only stroke our egos. He also speaks the truth to us, even when it's difficult for us to hear. He hones us, the way a knife is made sharper and more useful by being rubbed against another knife. And sometimes that can be painful!

Day 354
FIGHT SEGREGATION

You do well when you complete the Royal Rule of the Scriptures: "Love others as you love yourself." But if you play up to these so-called important people, you go against the Rule and stand convicted by it.

JAMES 2:8–9 MSG

❧

Jesus never ignored a leper coming to Him, even if the leper looked disgusting due to his disease. If He had thoughts of disgust when looking at a person, He always chose love. It's a good reminder that even when a person doesn't look or act like we want, we are still called to love.

Day 355
STAGES OF LIFE

---

*Like an open book, you watched me grow
from conception to birth; all the stages of
my life were spread out before you.*

PSALM 139:16 MSG

✑

If a cooking project has several steps involved, a
good chef will gather the supplies and organize
things before starting the actual cooking process.
God is like that too. Before we were born, He laid
out the various stages of our lives and purposefully
sorted them. There are no surprises or mysteries
to His plan. All of our stages or circumstances
of life are laid out before Him. It's time to
trust Him!

Day 356
SURRENDERED GIFTS

Every good gift and every perfect gift is from above, and comes down from the Father of lights, with whom there is no variation or shadow of turning.

JAMES 1:17 NKJV

～

Anything you have or enjoy that is positive and pleasant is from God. He is the only One with the capability and the nature to give these blessings. We humans cannot give them to ourselves. And Satan will never give us anything truly good, only things that look good to bait us.

Because we know the Giver, we can surrender our blessings back to Him.

Day 357
ENTERTAINING ANGELS

Do not neglect to show hospitality to strangers,
for by this some have entertained
angels without knowing it.

HEBREWS 13:2 NASB

In the New Testament, the Greek word translated *hospitality* literally means "love of strangers"—and the word for *angel* means "messenger." The author of Hebrews is telling us that it's not only our friends who bless us. Sometimes God sends strangers into our lives with a message we need to hear. Are our hearts open when we meet someone who seems different from us? Are we willing to hear God speaking through that person?

Day 358
GOD IS AT WORK

Even though on the outside it often looks like things are falling apart on us, on the inside, where God is making new life, not a day goes by without his unfolding grace.

2 CORINTHIANS 4:16 MSG

⌒

Every Christmas Eve as a child, I was excited to go to bed. I knew the presents under our Christmas tree would grow overnight. My parents worked to surprise me and my brother while I slept.

In the same way, you won't always see God at work, but as you trust Him, know change is on the way.

Day 359
HE IS OUR PROTECTOR

The LORD says, "I will rescue those who love me.
I will protect those who trust in my name."

PSALM 91:14 NLT

❧

Recently, my husband was hanging shelving in our garage when a piece pulled away from the wall. As a result, he crashed about four feet to the cement floor. Thanks to the metal shelving on the ground and the angels and grace of God, he walked away with only a bruised forearm and the need for a chiropractor visit.

Be at peace. God is watching over you and protecting your every step.

Day 360
FINDING OUT WHO WE ARE

It's in Christ that we find out who we are and what we are living for.

EPHESIANS 1:11 MSG

The two compelling questions for all mankind are: Who am I, and where am I going? Paul addresses the identity issue in his letter to the Ephesians. It is in Christ that we find out who we are and what we are here for. Our salvation involves so much more than just a ticket to heaven. Identifying with Christ affirms there are no accidents in life. We work as unto Him. We serve our families because of Him. We are who we are, because of Him.

Day 361
IT'S A PROCESS

*But grow in grace, and in the knowledge of
our Lord and Saviour Jesus Christ.*
2 PETER 3:18 KJV

The only thing that grows overnight is the beanstalk
in the fairy tale about the giant. In real life, growing
things involves a process.

It's the same with your journey in godly
womanhood. You must stay in the sunshine of
God's love and refuse to wilt in the rain. If you
stay connected to Him, the source of life, you
will grow into mature beauty.

Day 362
THE BEHAVIOR OF OLDER WOMEN

The aged women likewise, that they be in
behaviour as becometh holiness.
TITUS 2:3 KJV

⤳

In this passage, Paul is giving a litany of behavioral instructions for the people of God. He calls out character qualities for both older and younger men and women. To the older gals, he focuses in on their behavior or, literally, their position in society. They are exhorted to live a life that is holy or sacred. They are honorable. Their godliness was to set them apart. Does ours?

Day 363
REST IN PEACE

You will keep in perfect peace all who trust in you, all whose thoughts are fixed on you!

ISAIAH 26:3 NLT

❧

On a recent trip to my in-laws, my one-year-old was sleeping on the floor in the guest room. In the morning, I pulled him onto my tummy, and we laid there for another twenty minutes. He wasn't sleeping; neither was I. We were just resting. He knew he was safe in my arms.

God's unfathomable peace can be yours; find yourself a place where you can simply rest in His presence. There, you'll find peace.

Day 364
LIFE IS SHORT

For what is your life? It is even a vapour,
that appeareth for a little time,
and then vanisheth away.

JAMES 4:14 KJV

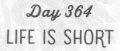

Regardless of our chronological age, it's helpful to remember that life is short. James compares life to a vapor and uses a term that refers to the exhalation of our breath. It is useful while it's in our body, but then it's exhaled and gone. Life is meant to be full and vibrant, but once it's gone, its usefulness is finished. So let's cherish these moments: hug our kids, love our husbands, and care for our coworkers. Do things that matter.

EVERLASTING LOVE

*"I have loved you, my people, with an
everlasting love. With unfailing love
I have drawn you to myself."*

JEREMIAH 31:3 NLT

God's love never ends. It never fails. It's unconditional. It's broader and deeper than anything we could ever comprehend because it has no limits, no boundary lines it refuses to cross. Wherever we go, it follows us. It pulls at our hearts because somewhere inside us all, we know God's love is the source of all our joy. God's everlasting love isn't a part of eternity. It *is* eternity.

Scripture Index

New Testament